I Just Want My Kids To Be Happy!

Why you shouldn't say it
Why you shouldn't think it
What you should embrace instead

Aaron Cooper, Ph.D. & Eric Keitel, M.Ed.

LATE AUGUST PRESS
CHICAGO

Published in the United States by Late August Press,
an imprint of Ace Coupay Publishing, Chicago.

www.mykidshappiness.com

Owing to limitations of space, all acknowledgments
to reprint previously published material may be found
at the end of the volume.

Publisher's Cataloging-in-Publication Data
Cooper, Aaron, 1951-
I just want my kids to be happy! : why you shouldn't say it,
why you shouldn't think it, what you should embrace
instead / Aaron Cooper, Eric Keitel.

p. cm.
Includes bibliographic references.
ISBN-13: 978-0-9797926-0-1   ISBN-10: 0-9797926-0-6
1. Child rearing.   2. Parenting.   3. Happiness.
4. Happy children.   I. Keitel, Eric.   II. Title.

HQ769.C66   2008
649'.2 -dc22   2007931947

This title may be purchased for business or promotional use
or for special sales. For information, please email:
aaroncooperphd@post.harvard.edu.

To Shawn,

who, at age 5, said,

"I'm thankful for parents who know

how to take good care of children."

Contents

PART THREE

TILLING THE SOIL OF AUTHENTIC HAPPINESS

"Let us be grateful to people who make us happy;

They are the charming gardeners

who make our souls blossom."

Marcel Proust

PART ONE

THE HAPPINESS DILEMMA

1

Every Parent's Mantra

"There is only one passion, the passion for happiness."
Denis Diderot

W hy are so many of our children so unhappy?
So worried.
So anxious.
So depressed.
Even youngsters who seem fine on the outside—good friends, good grades, a seemingly good life—may not be thriving on the inside. In a study conducted in the late 1990s, over half the surveyed ninth graders said they are "unhappy, sad or depressed." *Over half.* Three-quarters reported that it is "somewhat" or "very true" that they worry a lot.[1] The Centers for Disease Control issued a report in 2004 showing that 29% of high school students nationwide *felt so sad or hopeless* almost every day for at least two weeks that they stopped doing some of their usual activities.[2] That same survey found that 16% of students had made a plan to attempt suicide. College counseling centers report a substantial increase in the incidence of student mental health problems compared to twenty years ago.[3]

Why are so many young people in such distress? You'd expect just the opposite: our sons and daughters have more opportunities, more material advantages, and a greater array of personal freedoms than ever before. And yet, they feel so much unhappiness—despite growing up in an era when *the happiness of their children seems to be most parents' fondest wish.*

We hear it everywhere: *I just want them to be happy.* It's become a kind of mantra, a password into the not-so-secret society of concerned and loving elders, proud to assert what matters to them most. *I just want them to be happy.* Millions have pledged their allegiance to the happiness of their offspring while, paradoxically, kids are less happy than ever.

Is there a connection? Is it more than a statistical fluke, this inverse relationship between the happiness of young people and so many parents' commitment to their children's bliss? Could there be something about the happiness creed that invites this unintended result: children suffering rather than thriving in the face of life's daily challenges?

To the question, "Is there a connection?" we offer a resounding *Yes!* And while we recognize that complex social phenomena are often multi-determined, and thus a number of factors surely contribute to the disquieting state of our youth, we argue here that *I just want them to be happy* is one of the leading culprits.

Tell the truth: you're skeptical. You reached for this book with the confidence of Columbus after so many voyages, convinced that endorsing your children's happiness is as unassailable as the earth is round. What fault can possibly be found with a creed that has always sounded so right, so loving, so wonderfully free from the pressures of parental expectations—

around work, around family, around lifestyle—that have been felt by generations past? For as long as you can remember, you've heard *I just want them to be happy* trip off the lips of nearly every parent you know. And you've uttered it yourself—how many times?—with the quiet confidence we reserve for time-tested platitudes that are certain to invite the nodding of heads and the smiles of agreement.

Indeed, over the past twenty years, *I just want them to be happy* has become a kind of sacred star in the galaxy of parenting wisdom. When research psychologists ask groups of parents what they want for their children, happiness is the answer most often heard. The rich and famous, with their easy access to the media, trumpet the belief with the same confidence as the rest of us, lending the attitude even brighter currency. Dr. Phil, a guest on television's "Larry King Live" in September 2004, switched roles for a moment when he asked King to define success as applied to his children. "That they'd be happy," King replied without hesitation. And in an interview in *Parade* magazine in January 2006, actress Sarah Jessica Parker was asked what kind of future she wished for her son. "I'd like him to be an educated person and make contributions that are important," she said. "But honestly? I'd rather have him happy than smart or successful. I just want happiness for him."

This near-religious devotion to our children's happiness ought not to surprise anyone. After all, it's a belief rooted deep in the American soul for over 200 years, since the Declaration of Independence asserted certain unalienable rights, including life, liberty, and *the pursuit of happiness*. For centuries, immigrants have flocked to our shores to partake of the bounty that might produce happiness and a better life for them and, more importantly, *for their children.*

But generations past didn't speak of happiness as we do now; they didn't esteem it as an ultimate end in itself. In preparing this book, we asked men and women beyond fifty years of age what they remember hearing their parents and grandparents talk about as *the most important thing,* their centerpiece wish for their offspring. We asked people of different ethnic, racial and religious backgrounds, people who were born in the United States as well as abroad. Our informal survey turned up many things; happiness was rarely among them:

- I want them to be healthy.
- I want them to be productive.
- I want them to find a good husband/wife.
- I want them to make a contribution.
- I want them to have long life.
- I want them to have good children.
- I want them to have peace of mind.

The farther back memory went, the less likely anyone was to recollect the happiness message. It's a development of the late twentieth century, and now, in the new millennium, we're hearing it more than ever.

Why is this so? Why have millions eagerly embraced this one particular attitude?

Like any popular trend in belief or behavior, no one explanation fits all. We offer some possibilities:

The culture of affluence during the past few decades, with its emphasis on convenience, speed, and ease, seems to have shaped, for many, the illusion that *all* of life—the emotional as well as the practical—can and ought to be easy and pleasurable and pain-free. But it's nothing more than an illusion, and *I just want them to be happy* a rallying cry for so many wishful thinkers. Life has rarely been emotionally easy, whether one is affluent or not. As we will see later, there is no pain-free route to authentic happiness, despite the allure of one seductive creed.

Affluence isn't the only change to have marked the cultural landscape in the past thirty years. Whereas generations past put their faith in family, marriage, work, and religion—what many parents used to value *most of all*—moms and dads these days bring an understandable skepticism to these once-trustworthy institutions. Family? Over the past four decades, geographic mobility has split families apart; physical distance has loosened sibling connections. Marriage? Once regarded as the tie that binds, divorce rates over 50% have brought a jolt of reality to the fantasy of wedded bliss. Career? Change is the buzzword as workers face unexpected layoffs, exchange one employer for another, and pursue second or third careers. Organized religion has taken its hits with scandal and fraud, and leadership caught in all manner of hypocrisy. When family, marriage, career and church can no longer be assumed to offer pathways to happiness, parents are left expressing only *the wish*, hoping their sons and daughters will somehow find *the way*.

Others utter *I just want them to be happy* as a kind of prayer, an incantation against what they fear: that our harried, pressured lifestyles may be shortchanging children of the attention and parental involvement that kids need. With moms and dads exhausted at the end of the day, with many single parents juggling it all, and with so many of us mindlessly chasing the buck on a consumer treadmill—who's nurturing the kids? On a deep level, many fear that their sons and daughters won't be all right.

Some embrace the happiness creed as a badge of enlightened broad-mindedness, an acknowledgement that many paths lead to a contented life and "I can't presume to know what's right for you." This may be especially true for Boomer and post-Boomer (Generation X) parents, raised or influenced by Depression-era elders who preached economic security above all else. Some Boomers and Gen Xers refuse to do the same, priding themselves instead on conveying to their own offspring an expanded sense of possibilities. Not a repudiation of achievement exactly, but something more than the narrow parameters that were prescribed for them.[4]

For others, the endorsement of the happiness creed reflects a certain disenchantment with their own material lifestyles. Despite their economic advantages, many parents face loneliness, disillusionment, a kind of spiritual malaise. They sense that something is missing in their lives that money cannot buy. So they embrace the happiness creed in the hope that their children will attain what they have not.

And finally, there are the parents for whom *I just want them to be happy* is merely the politically correct thing to say, while other words and actions reveal so much more. Sure they want their kids to be content, but they believe the way to get there is through achievement, wealth or status—Harvard or Yale on the brain. And so the mantra is a kind of veil obscuring the pressures for excellence, even perfection, which many of these parents impose.

As a psychologist (Cooper) and an educator (Keitel), we've been tracking the trajectory of the happiness creed in the counseling office and the classroom for nearly thirty years. Here's a sampling of what we have heard:

Consider 12-year-old Jennifer, a girl who is struggling unsuccessfully to make friends and to find entrée into the cliquish world of her suburban middle school. Her mother laments the disappointments her daughter has faced, and has made Jennifer's struggle her own. She coaxes her daughter to try new and varied solutions, and has created, in the process, a level of tension between the two of them that has become its own thorny dilemma. "Isn't it my responsibility to see that my daughter is happy?" the mother asks, wiping away tears.

Consider Luke, a high school junior with a history of poor grades and an indifferent attitude toward responsibility. Despite all of that, his parents bought him a car, a decision they explained by describing how upset Luke felt being one of the few boys "without wheels" in their affluent suburban neighborhood. "I just want him to be happy," said Luke's father.

And consider 12-year-old Ann, who has become obsessed with her looks, her body, and fashion. She travels in a crowd that wears the latest styles and she's frequently pushing her mother to take her to the mall. "I don't have the kind of money to allow her to keep up with her friends," Ann's mother says, "but somehow, I guess because I want her to be happy, we're always bringing home something new for her to wear. My credit card bill is through the roof."

And yet, despite parents' efforts to nurture their children's happiness, *our youth appear less happy than ever*. A 2006 survey commissioned by *Family Circle* magazine found that 27% of American teens—ten million kids—report being "unhappy or just okay."[5]

And what of the future of this generation? Will they be as happy in their adult lives as the generations that preceded them? Since 1972, the Pew Research Center has been surveying adult Americans to find out how happy we are as a nation. The numbers have remained stable for over three decades: about a third of respondents report being "very happy," another half "pretty happy."[6] It's easy to fear that the numbers will change, that our unhappy youth will become a generation less content, less thriving than those that have come before them—despite their parents' widespread endorsement of the happiness creed.

Or, perhaps, because of it—because there's something about *the way parents have applied the happiness creed*, and the way youth have interpreted their parents' endorsement of that creed during the last 20 to 30 years, that is contributing to the problems of young people today. In particular, we will argue that *I just want them to be happy* leads well-intentioned mothers and fathers astray in their child-rearing practices, ultimately undermining the ability of young people to face the challenges of life with balance, resilience, and imagination. We will argue that it produces materially and emotionally indulged kids, ill-equipped to cope in a world that turns no somersaults for any one person's happiness. We will offer, instead, an evidence-based roadmap that parents can follow to guide their children toward the contented, happy life that is every parent's dream.

We're not happiness-bashers. We're not opposed to living lives of contentment and well-being. There's no denying that happiness is a good thing; research and our intuition attest to that. But something troubling has resulted from the way contemporary families have put into practice the eternal desire to see their children thrive. And therein lies the dilemma: how to pursue a worthy goal without going awry. We argue, in this book, that *I just want them to be happy* has become the leading obstacle in our children's way, impeding their stride toward that grand destination, and bringing about instead the very outcomes loving parents hope to avoid.

But first, let's take a closer look at what we mean when we use the word *happiness,* and what it has meant through the ages.

2

Happiness in Perspective

"All men seek happiness. This is without exception.
Whatever different means they employ, they all
tend to this end."

Blaise Pascal

There's no shortage of research corroborating what we
know intuitively—that happiness is a good thing. Studies have found that happy people live longer, healthier,
and more engaged lives, are more altruistic and less preoccupied with themselves.

> "If you're happy, you're more likely to initiate social
> contact with friends. You're more likely to respond positively when others ask you for help. You're less likely
> to suffer from psychosomatic illnesses—digestive disorders, other stress disorders, headaches, vascular
> stress. You're less likely to be absent from work or to
> get involved in disputes at work. And you're less likely
> to attempt suicide—the ultimate behavioral measure of
> unhappiness." [7]

Some scientists say that the pursuit of happiness has been a mechanism responsible for our survival as a species, motivating us for thousands of years toward tasty food and warm shelter and the pleasures of sex—all the "feel good" fundamentals. It remains, today, our core motivator.

Although we talk about happiness all the time, it isn't easy to define. The Oxford American Dictionary defines happy as "feeling or showing *pleasure* or *contentment*" (italics ours).

Pleasure or contentment—two very different things.

Pleasure tends to be a fleeting sensation, involving the senses and what some call the "positive" emotions. Pleasure results from a particular experience: an appetizing meal, a good massage, an engaging movie, satisfying sex. *Contentment*, on the other hand, connotes a longer stretch of time, an over-arching sense of subjective well-being. The contented person is someone satisfied with life *as a whole*.

As a parent, which dimension of happiness do you have in mind—pleasure or contentment—when you think, or say, *I just want them to be happy*? Are you referring to your child's short-term happiness (how they feel today and tomorrow), or long-term happiness (how they will feel in the future)? Perhaps you are thinking of both.

We've asked many parents what they mean when they say these words. Our question often gives pause; many have never reflected on that simple platitude. Some say it's a life free of pain and suffering:

- "I don't want my kids to be stressed out."
- "I want them to have little hardship."
- "I want things to be going well for them."

- "I don't want them to be upset or sad."
- "I want to see them smiling."

Others define happiness as a life of desires satisfied and personal goals fulfilled:

- "I want them to be all that they can be, to realize their potential."
- "I hope there are no insurmountable obstacles in their way."
- "I want them to have whatever their heart desires."

Some parents tell us that happiness means career success, with the comforts and financial security that career success brings. "My lifestyle has a lot to do with my happiness," one father explained. "I'd like my kids to have the same advantages someday that I have."

And others tell us that they don't know what will bring their children happiness, but they have confidence that it's attainable.

In *The Childhood Roots of Adult Happiness*, psychiatrist Edward Hallowell explains happiness as "a feeling that your life is going well."[8] Does he literally mean a "feeling," a transient emotion? (Feelings are constantly changing: I get out of bed feeling *happy*, find myself *frustrated* and *upset* an hour later during a terrible commute to work, then *satisfied* and *proud* an hour after that when my boss gives me a favorable quarterly review.) Surely Hallowell doesn't have in mind the "pleasure" kind of happiness, as if life were a series of smiley-face episodes. He must be referring to the "contentment" part of the dictionary definition, a sense that life *as a whole* is going well. Does it mean that our lives are free of pain? Not necessarily. Most people recognize that life inevitably includes times of emotional pain and suffering, but that overall satisfaction is possible nevertheless. Even the most idealistic parents, the ones who ardently endorse *I just want them to be happy*, know that solid lives can't be formed, like pearls on a string, out of a succession of pleasurable moments.

The historical view of happiness has taken some interesting turns. Coming from the Old Norse word, *happ*, meaning chance or luck, happiness in its earliest western expression was considered a gift of the gods, beyond the reach of ordinary mortals to influence or control. (Think of words like *happen*stance and per*haps*.) A shift in thinking took place during classical times, when Aristotle proposed that everyone was motivated toward achieving happiness, and that happiness was tied to virtue. The happy person, according to Aristotle, was the one who relied on his intellect to lead him to virtuous acts. It was no longer a question of luck or chance; happiness depended on how people used their minds and conducted themselves in the world.

Eastern philosophy also assigned the mind a central role in the attainment of happiness, but in a very different way. Early Buddhist teachers regarded happiness as the absence of suffering, and proposed that through the development of a *conscious* mind—achieving wisdom, seeking tranquility, practicing compassion—people could learn to detach from their suffering; happiness would result.

Centuries later, medieval Christianity brought a certain sensual element into the mix by viewing happiness as the endless pleasures of eternal bliss awaiting us in the afterlife, provided we lived the virtuous life on earth. Our actions still mattered, but happiness wasn't likely to be attainable until later, in heaven.

By the late seventeenth century, the seeds of our current hedonistic view of happiness were sown by Enlightenment philosophers such as John Locke, who viewed happiness as the result of pleasure. Feeling good replaced being good in defining happiness.[9] And no longer was there one agreed-upon formula for attaining happiness, whether drawn from religious or secular thought. It became a personal thing, a democratic approach: happiness as the expression of each of our unique destinies; your source of happiness isn't necessarily mine.

Today, it is an assumption of modern life that attaining happiness is within everyone's power.[10] We may each ultimately find our bliss on a path that is uniquely our own; it's viewed as a kind of birthright, our potential to achieve happiness.

The contemporary era brings something to the happiness discourse that has never been seen before: empirical research. For the first time in recorded history, our understanding of happiness isn't limited to what religious scholars and secular philosophers have to say. Large segments of populations have been studied in the past thirty years, allowing us to understand happiness in a new way. Research in the fields of social science, neuroscience, psychiatry, and economics has enabled us to identify the underpinnings of the happy life *as people actually live it*. Nowadays, we're not just speculating about the ingredients that shape happy lives: we have a pretty good idea who is happy, and why. And we're able to say that

16

the Enlightenment seems to have gotten it wrong: the road to happiness doesn't traverse the field of earthly delights. The pursuit of pleasures is not the way.

What is the road to a happy life? How can parents help their children attain authentic happiness and not just transient pleasures? To answer these questions, we reviewed a great deal of empirical research into the factors that allow some fortunate people to enjoy lives of contentment and well-being. We searched for patterns in the data, factors that turned up again and again. Through our review, we have identified *eight elements* that most reliably predict who is happy and who is not.

In addition, we reviewed the writings of practitioners—psychologists and teachers and others who work with children and adults—plus the writings of child development theorists, the experts who study the life cycle from birth to maturity. From this literature, we have culled *five dimensions* of home life that can tilt the happiness odds in your kids' favor.

Finally, we assembled all this into a blueprint for happiness, a child-rearing approach that conceives of parents as gardeners, planting the right *seeds* (the eight elements) and tilling a nutrient-rich *soil* (the five dimensions of home life) so that their children's lives can bloom into gardens of authentic happiness.

But first there's the clearing of the land, pulling the weeds that threaten to strangle the garden's growth. The most invasive weed: *I just want them to be happy.*

3

The Happiness Creed:
Why You Shouldn't Say It

"Careful the things you say
Children will listen
Careful the things you do
Children will see and learn
Children may not obey
But children will listen."
Stephen Sondheim[11]

Our children are listening.

We think they're not. We think they're absorbed in the world of iPods and instant messaging, skateboards and The Simpsons. We think that because they turn a deaf ear when we ask them to hang up their clothes or finish their homework, they're not paying attention to what we say.

We're wrong about that.

Author and educator Dennis Prager suggests that parents ask their kids this question: "What do you think is most important to me: that you be smart, successful, happy, or good?" The answer, Prager says, tells parents which one of these four values their kids are absorbing most from the messages they receive at home.[12]

We asked the question in the course of preparing this book—not a scientific sampling, but an informal survey of nearly one hundred middle school students at an independent day school on Chicago's North Side.[13]

The question: If you asked my parent(s), they would say that the most important thing is that I grow up to be:

- smart
- successful
- happy
- good

Seventy percent of the students selected "happy," followed by "successful" (18%), "good" (8%), and "smart" (4%).

It's no accident that *happy* was the overwhelming choice; our kids hear us utter the happiness creed all the time. They hear us say it to their teachers, to our friends and relatives, to other parents, and to them.

Unfortunately, it's a message that fails them in five ways:

- We're overemphasizing pleasure.
- We're promoting unrealistic expectations.
- We're fostering guilt and shame.
- We're encouraging too much self-focus.
- We're telling a half-truth.

Let's examine each of these in turn.

We're overemphasizing pleasure

What does the concept of happiness mean in the mind of a youngster? Do children understand the word in the way adults intend it?

Until about age twelve, children's thinking tends to be what the developmental psychologist Jean Piaget called *concrete*: things are only what they are in the material, tangible world, never symbols of anything else. The moon is an orb in the sky, not a symbol of romance; the owl is a bird, not a symbol of wisdom. Happy? It means fun or pleasure—nothing more. Not contentment, not overall well-being. Ask a youngster if he's happy and he'll say "yes" if *at that moment* he's enjoying playing with a toy, engaged by television, or munching on his favorite snack.

It's only after age 12 or 13, when the mind matures into *abstract* thinking, that happiness can come to symbolize the condition of overall well-being, of life satisfaction in general. And yet, many of the teens we've spoken to, like the younger kids, still seem to regard happiness as a series of uninterrupted pleasures. Others express a slightly different understanding that reflects the narcissistic self-centeredness of adolescence: they interpret *I just want them to be happy* as less about fun and more about having one's way. Whether it's convincing a parent to extend the curfew, receiving an invitation to the school dance, or making an "A" on an important exam, happiness, for these teens, means getting what they want in life.

In other words, few children, regardless of their age, have the capacity to differentiate fun (or pleasure) from contentment, to understand that fun is temporary while contentment is ongoing, that fun is *during* while contentment extends into *after*.[14] If confusing pleasure with happiness is an inevitable error of the young mind, we only reinforce that erroneous way of thinking when our kids hear us give voice to the happiness creed. (What should they hear us say instead? By the end of this book, you will know the answer.)

But the problem is greater than seven simple words. Mistaking pleasure for authentic happiness isn't limited to our youth anymore. As a society, we have come to embrace all kinds of shortcuts to happiness—easy pleasures instead of more enduring gratifications. "Every wealthy nation creates more and more shortcuts to pleasure," writes psychologist Martin Seligman, "television, drugs, shopping, loveless sex, spectator sports, and chocolate to name just a few." [15] As we pursue these happiness-substitutes as though they were "the real thing," our children are watching, learning, and imitating us. *I just want them to be happy* only reinforces, in our youngsters' minds, the notion that shortcuts are the way to go. Seligman suggests that the rising rates of depression in this country—youth and adult—may be associated with our increased reliance on so many shortcuts.

Life will never offer our children the uninterrupted flow of fun and pleasure that the happiness creed encourages them to desire.

We're promoting unrealistic expectations

We do our kids a great disservice by emphasizing happiness when life promises they'll encounter so much more.

When we say, "I just want you to be happy," what are we implying about the other human emotions? What are we implying about sadness? About disappointment? About hurt, anger, or fear? When our kids hear us talk as though happiness were the most important feeling of all, they receive the message that these other feelings are undesirable or second-class—feelings to be avoided.

Not a good message for our children to take away.

In the course of each day, the emotions—a great many emotions—come and go like the weather, naturally and spontaneously. It's supposed to be that way. Psychologist Daniel Gilbert suggests that nature designed us *not* to be happy all the time, that our emotions are a signaling system sending us important information as we go about our lives.[16] If only happiness stirred in our hearts, we'd be at a great disadvantage trying to steer ourselves down the road of life.

One of parenting's most important tasks is helping kids develop a level of comfort with *all* feelings—so they know not to fear them, not to critique them, and not to turn away from them. *I just want them to be happy* sends the opposite message: it conveys that some feelings are good and others bad, some to be sought after and others avoided.

Parents would do better to teach their children Buddhism's First Noble Truth: all life includes suffering. Can any among us say we haven't known the pain of sadness, upset, hurt or disappointment? Can any among us say we haven't encountered troubling events that we could not alter or control? More helpful to our children than only extolling happiness is teaching them about the inevitability of life's rough times, and teaching them how to be at ease with the full spectrum of emotions.

Suppose your nine-year-old son's best friend moves hundreds of miles away. How might your son feel? Sadness would be appropriate—and not just for ten or twenty minutes, but on and off for weeks. Wouldn't it be wonderful if he could express his sadness, talk about how he misses his friend and wishes they were still together? Wouldn't it be wonderful if he could feel as comfortable talking about his sadness as he might feel talking about happiness or excitement or joy? His capacity to express his feelings depends largely on the lessons he's learning at home: whether you model a healthy, balanced expression of your own sadness, and how you react when he expresses his. If you only want him to be happy, you may transmit the message that sadness isn't okay to feel and express, that sadness isn't something you want to see!

Suppose your 11-year-old daughter discovers she's been excluded from a neighborhood club formed by a group of her classmates. How might she feel? Perhaps hurt and disappointed, perhaps upset and sad. In the complex web of interpersonal relations, all these feelings are inevitable. Wouldn't it be wonderful if she could accept all her feelings, talk about them and know by your supportive reaction that her feelings are legitimate and appropriate—every bit as legitimate and appropriate as happiness?

> "The hardest lesson I have had to learn as a parent is to allow any of my children to be unhappy. At first, I felt I had to wipe their unhappy feelings away, as if I were a large roll of Bounty paper towels and my children's

unhappy feelings were a spill in need of sponging. But [my wife] set me straight. She told me that if I didn't ever allow our kids to say they felt unhappy, then they would get the message that I never wanted to hear about their unhappy feelings. And I knew that would be a big problem. As your children come to know that you can tolerate their feeling unhappy, they will be more likely to tell you how they feel. This is all you really need."[17]

A few words about feelings...

Feelings—they're never good, they're never bad. They're never right or wrong. They are simply *information*—about how we're reacting to people ("I'm *hurt* by the way she's talking to me"); about how we're reacting to events ("I'm *proud* and *thrilled* to be at my son's graduation"); about how we're reacting to our own private thoughts and imaginings ("I'm *sad* remembering the hard times around the divorce").

Feelings are not necessarily "truth"; they can trick and mislead us. That's why feelings should never be worshipped, never elevated to a loftier place than they deserve as a simple thermometer of our emotional life. Not a thermometer of the world, nor of reality; not to be equated with "truth."

The idea that feelings aren't a reliable gauge of reality is surprising and confusing to many people. Consider this example: I walk onto an airplane and feel a surge of fear. What does it mean, this fear? Is there something to be afraid of? Should I treat it as a kind of "truth" about flying? Probably not; air travel is relatively safe. Because feelings are information, it makes sense to *confront our feelings with our intelligence* in order to de-cipher their meaning. It makes sense to ask ourselves, *What's up with me* that I'm feeling this way? Perhaps, as I walked onto the plane, I noticed the scent of gasoline, which triggered my fear. Is there a leak? Perhaps I've spotted a passenger suspiciously fiddling with what seem to be wires under his sweater, which triggered my fear. Is she a terrorist? Perhaps I've recently read an article describing the poor air quality on passenger planes, and the contents of that article lurk in the back of my mind. Is the flight going to compromise my health? Or maybe I'm ex-periencing a "flashback" feeling, an *old* fear of flying that I thought I had fully overcome, and so my feelings have more to do with the past than with the present. Only the mind's careful reflection can answer the question, *What's up with me?* And even then, we can't always decipher our emotions; even after careful scrutiny we sometimes remain baffled.

Since the 1995 publication of Daniel Goleman's *Emo-tional Intelligence*,[18] there's been a popular literature asserting that emotional intelligence is more important than general in-telligence in predicting success in life. What is emotional in-telligence? It's the mix of inborn talents and learned skills that enable us to get along and deal effectively with others, and to operate with a certain awareness of our emotional selves. Stud-ies have demonstrated that people with high emotional intelli-gence tend to be more successful in life. What can parents do to promote emotional intelligence in children? Teach them to ask themselves, "What's up with me?" (What am I feeling and where is it coming from?) Being able to name feelings ("I'm upset." "I'm sad." "I'm excited." "I'm afraid.") is the skill that all the other elements of emotional intelligence require.[19] That's one skill that affords youngsters a big advantage in achieving a happy life.

We're fostering guilt and shame

Parents say *I just want you to be happy.* But let's imagine what's it like for our kids when, for whatever reason, they're not feeling so sunny inside.

"It really freaks my mother out when I'm unhappy," says Kimberly, a seventh-grader. "I can tell by the look on her face. She gets all concerned and asks me what's wrong, what's wrong. If I don't give her an answer, she keeps asking and looks at me real funny, like she's gonna cry. *I feel so bad* when she gets that look on her face."

Children discover, to their dismay, that happiness is elusive, unpredictable, and transitory. It comes and goes, can't be counted on to last. And yet many we've spoken to believe they should always be happy. They've heard their parents give voice to the happiness creed so many times that when other feelings pop up, they feel guilty for letting their parents down. Many blame themselves and think they're doing something wrong. Wishing not to disappoint their parents, some of these kids—girls are especially susceptible to this—plaster a smile across their faces regardless of how they're feeling inside. The smile is a mask, concealing their true emotions. It's a mask that isolates them from others just when they need to be seen for who they really are, when they need to talk about whatever is

26

unsettling in their hearts and minds. Too many parents have come to mistake the mask for the real thing, deluding themselves into thinking that their children are fine when they are not, that their children are happy when they may, in fact, be worried, anxious, or depressed. (Kids, too, can come to believe that the mask they wear is the reality they live; counselors encounter such children all the time, unaware and out of touch with their true feelings.)

Many of the kids we've spoken to sense that their happiness functions as a kind of reflection of their parents' success, an emblem of the family's luster ("We're doing well, there's no unhappiness here!") It's a weighty responsibility for young people, going through life as a walking, talking barometer of a parent's effectiveness.

> After weeks of noticing that 15-year-old Rebecca was daydreaming in class, rarely following along or turning in assignments, the teacher phoned home. Rebecca's mother revealed that an older sister had been diagnosed the month before with a life-threatening illness. "Rebecca seems fine around the house," the mother said cheerfully. "She's not the kind of girl who will let something like this get her down." The teacher knew from past meetings with the mother that her children's happiness was "the most important thing." Loyal to the family style, Rebecca refused to let her mother or sister witness her sadness or upset or fear. She bottled up her emotions at home, while at school drifted into episodes of daydreaming. She acknowledged how guilty she'd feel letting her mother see her so unhappy.

But even tougher than guilt—more crippling, more undermining—is shame. It's the feeling triggered when our inner voice says, "Something is wrong with me. I'm no good. I don't have what it takes." We've heard these words too many times from kids distraught over their *inability to be happy*. They have come to see themselves as defective because they can't fulfill their parents' most important wish. (Of course, no child can.) It's rarely easy to convince these suffering youngsters that the problem resides not in them but in their parents' allegiance to one misguided creed.

We're encouraging too much self-focus

I just want them to be happy transmits to our kids that *their* emotional life is the most important thing—more than family, community, country, planet. It transmits that *their* personal welfare trumps everything else. But do we want to encourage in our children a sense that they are the center of the universe?

In so many ways, the culture in recent decades has promoted a preoccupation with self. Too many parents, beyond giving children the love and attention that they require, seem to have gone overboard in elevating their kids to a kind of celebrity status in the home—pampering and indulging them and catering to every whim. It was one thing, in the past, for a child to keep a diary, a personal record for *private* reflection. Today, the diary goes online—we call it a blog—and millions of young people (as well as adults) operate from the assumption that the world is interested in *their* thoughts and feelings.

Technology alone does not account for this trend; a prevailing attitude of self-focus and self-absorption is necessary to grease the Internet's wheels.

Life as the center of the universe might play at home for a handful of years, but there's a rude awakening in store once our kids venture into the world. Out there, the sun won't rise and set on their every whim and fancy; out there, others won't be devoted to their happiness in the way mom and dad might have been.

There are times when we need to put others first if we want to succeed—in marriage, at work, in the community. There are times we need to compromise, even to sacrifice our immediate happiness for some greater good. Yet many parents cater to their children—put their youngsters' wishes first—to keep the kids happy. The result, in the end, is children ill-prepared for a world where their personal needs and wants won't always be paramount to the people around them.

For parents devoted to the happiness creed, it's especially challenging when their own needs bump up against the needs of the kids. Or when the needs of the family *as a group* conflict with the needs of the child *as an individual*. These parents tend to feel guilty when they put themselves or the family first, when they say, "No, you can't go out tonight. We're all having dinner together." Or, "You won't be able to play soccer on Saturday. We're going to Grandma's birthday party." Or, "No, I won't chauffeur you across town to see your friends. I've had a very hard day and I'm exhausted." Looks of disappointment and indignation on the faces of so many sons and daughters—*How can you deny me? Isn't my happiness the most important thing?*—persuade parents to capitulate. When *I just want them to be happy* holds sway, who pays the price? Everyone. The children develop an over-inflated sense of their own importance, and a sense of entitlement, while the needs and desires of mom and dad and the family get pushed aside.

Research shows that children are busier these days than in decades past: after-school lessons, formal play dates, sports and activities fill all available hours. Is it because there are more opportunities for kids to partake of? Perhaps. But we also see a willingness by parents to fill every waking hour so that children don't suffer boredom, don't feel left out, don't languish unhappily on the personal development vine.

In 1952, Americans were asked whether they thought people lived "as good lives—honest and moral—as they used to." Half of the respondents said yes, half said no. By 1998, only a quarter of respondents said yes.[20] Something important had changed over the course of forty-six years: the perception (if not the reality) that others act more often from their own self-interest than out of respect for ethical standards and conventions, the foundation of a moral society. Does this survey reflect *real* social change? Are people less concerned about others than they once were? Are we quicker to "bend the rules" when it affords a personal advantage? It's been said that since the dawn of the "Me Generation" in the seventies, there's been little sign of "Us." *I just want them to be happy* may be one element of many paving our selfish way.

We're telling a half-truth

Eleanor, age seven, spends her summer days catching insects in jars. After she fills the jars, she tortures the bugs: pulls the legs off some, drowns others under a rush of water. She looks to be having a terrific time, and when asked, declares herself happy.

Julio, age thirteen, is a TV junkie: hours and hours of television after school and on weekends. When asked, he says he's happy glued to the tube, which he refers to as his hobby.

Many parents would find Eleanor and Julio's behavior unacceptable, despite the youngsters' claims to happiness. Few parents allow their kids total freedom to pursue what makes them happy. When we disapprove of our kids' behavior, even though they're happy doing what they're doing, most of us intervene: we put a stop to it, or we try, in subtle ways, to redirect their interest. In other words, not everything that gives them happiness meets with our approval. Not everything is acceptable to us, or even tolerated. And so *I just want them to be happy* tells only half the story; *doing what I think is best* tells the rest.

Actively influencing a child's choices and interests and tastes is a necessary part of being a good parent; we shouldn't passively sit by if our kids head down a bad path and start making dangerous choices. But parental influence can be destructive if it stifles a child's authentic (and healthy) self, quashing innate talents or interests or pressuring a child to be or do what she cannot. It's a situation observed frequently in affluent, privileged homes, and in homes that, regardless of economics, exert tremendous pressures toward achievement and excellence.[21] Not all children can excel, and a parent's wish won't make it so. Combine unrealistic parental pressures with the happiness creed and you have one confused, even troubled, youngster. What these kids would say, if they were able, is: "My parents want me to be happy, but their expectations and de-

31

mands leave me feeling like a failure—angry and upset and sad." It's a dilemma for these kids: they sense that they should-n't speak out, shouldn't talk about their distress because re-vealing their unhappiness betrays the all-important creed. So they go underground with their feelings, suppressing or hid-ing them until symptoms erupt—depression or anxiety—that cannot be hidden or denied.

In this chapter, we have discussed five ways that *I just want them to be happy* is the wrong message for parents to con-vey:

- We're overemphasizing pleasure.
- We're promoting unrealistic expectations.
- We're fostering guilt and shame.
- We're encouraging too much self-focus.
- We're telling a half-truth.

Children who grow up within earshot of these damaging mes-sages pay no small price, but they are not alone. Parents, as we will now see, also pay a price when they carry around the mis-taken notion that their children's happiness is the most impor-tant thing.

4

The Happiness Creed:
Why You Shouldn't Think It

"First thing we're gonna do," Coach Wingo told 16-year-old Bernard, "is follow certain forms and courtesies. You'll do whatever I tell you to do, and you'll do it with enthusiasm. I'm going to teach you to play football, and I'm going to teach you well. I'm going to run your ass off everyday, and after I run you till you drop, make you lift weights till you can't move, make you tackle till your arms cramp, something's gonna happen to you that's never happened to you in your miserable little life. You're going to be happy, kid."

Pat Conroy and Becky Johnston[22]

Thought tends to precede action.[23] Much of what we do begins with an idea, a belief. And it's our beliefs that shape our view of the world and influence the way we respond to people and events.

I just want them to be happy is more than just a wish. It's also a belief: that our kids' happiness is the most important thing. And that belief has five negative consequences—impacting our behavior and our feelings—that undermine our children's welfare:

- We're captive to our children's moods.
- We feel unnecessary guilt and shame when our kids aren't happy.
- We abdicate parental authority rather than cause our kids unhappiness.
- We overprotect our children from valuable encounters with adversity.
- We emphasize feelings over actions.

Let's examine each of these in turn.

We're captive to our children's moods

Kids are clever. They know where we're vulnerable. They know how to manipulate us to achieve certain ends. Where *I just want them to be happy* is the prevailing belief, they manipulate us by looking glum and wearing the face of sadness. They know we'll want to see a smile restored, a mood brightened.

> "If I look really, really sad," says 11-year-old Stephanie, "my mother asks me what's wrong. I know she doesn't like it when I'm unhappy. That's when I can get her to take me to the mall and buy me something. Even if she said I can't have a new blouse or jeans, she'll change her mind if I act very sad."

Even our youngest children learn quickly how to pull our strings. Four-year-old Hannah, sent to her room for a time-out after being naughty, cracked open the door after several minutes to shout down the hall, "I'm very *unhappy* right now!" She knew where her mother was vulnerable.

Of course, many children don't manipulate like this, which doesn't mean that parents won't transform into the happiness police anyway. The belief alone—that children should be happy—influences parents to become hyper-alert to every sadness, hurt, or disappointment, and eager to wipe away a frown. One result is parents gratifying their children's insatiable material desires, lest a son or daughter suffer unhappiness without the latest toys and gadgets and trendy fashions, the stuff all the other kids have. We've witnessed parents supporting their children's non-stop wishes to go and do and see and participate without restraint, just to keep the kids happy. Mothers in particular describe their exhaustion from life on a kind of hamster's wheel, always on the move, racing the kids to after-school lessons, to play dates at the homes of friends, to the mall for that last-minute purchase before the slumber party or the school dance. For many families, keeping the kids happy has gotten severely out of hand.

> "I know it sounds stupid," says a mother of two teens, "but it never occurred to me until now that I have a choice, that I don't have to say yes every time the girls ask me to chauffeur them somewhere. It seems like that's all I do on the weekends—drive them, pick them up, drop them off… Maybe it's because they look so unhappy when I turn them down."

35

Worshipping at the altar of happiness can render some parents unable or unwilling to acknowledge when their child is emotionally down. "I just didn't let myself see it," said one father about his son's depression. "I didn't want to believe that Matt was so unhappy." It's not uncommon for young people to say that their parents ignored or denied their feelings when they tried to tell them about their *unhappiness*.[24] Perhaps it's just too painful for some parents, brainwashed by the creed. For girls, who feel increasing pressures to be "perfect," to be successful and emotionally balanced and pleasing to the people around them,[25] a false smile goes undetected in the face of this parental blind spot. Unhappy boys also escape detection when the mask they hide behind is one of the traditional emblems of masculinity: the refusal to show emotion. Rather than feeling relieved by sharing their distress (and receiving support), kids in such isolation tend to grow increasingly troubled.

We feel unnecessary guilt and shame

We described the way so many kids feel guilty and ashamed when they fail to meet their parents' happiness expectations. There's a flip side to that phenomenon: parents feeling guilty and ashamed when their children aren't happy enough. *I just want them to be happy* has led many caring moms and dads to believe it's their responsibility to guarantee a son or daughter's sunny mood. And when the sun doesn't shine, these parents take quite a tumble.

It's natural to wish we had the power to set a protective shield around our kids' emotional lives, to insulate them from pain and suffering. But so much happens, good and bad, beyond our influence and control—with peers, with teachers and siblings, in the random unfoldings of the community and the larger world. Yet we've seen parents operate as though it was their job to manage and control their kids' moment-to-moment happiness.

> The mother of 13-year-old Haley seemed to be drowning in guilt as she spoke about her daughter's "blue moods." For weeks, the mother explained, Haley seemed listless and tired, without her usual interest in friends. When asked if there had been any recent changes or setbacks in Haley's life, she reported that she and her husband had decided on a separation; he had already moved out. We conjectured that Haley might simply be grieving this big loss. "I was afraid you'd say that," the mother said, deep lines forming across her brow. "I don't think I can bear to see her this way, on account of what her father and I have done."

The challenge of good parenting is tough enough for even the most skilled and devoted parents without our heaping needless guilt and shame onto ourselves the way Haley's mother does in our example. It's a burden we easily take on when we believe that it falls to us to assure our children's happiness.

We abdicate parental authority

As parents, we have to say "no." We have to know when to say it, we have to say it often, and we have to say it like we mean it. Without "no," children can't develop self-control. (We discuss self-control again in Chapter 7, but address it here first because *I just want them to be happy* is one of the obstacles preventing parents from saying "no.")

Self-control develops when kids begin to repeat to themselves—it's their inner voice talking—the limit-setting words they've heard their parents say to them. "No, you can't climb onto the table." "No, it's time to turn off the television and go to bed." "No, you're too young for a 1am curfew."

No matter how unhappy it makes our kids, we must say "no." Limit-setting is arguably the toughest part of parenting; few of us enjoy creating conditions that elicit our sons' and daughters' unhappiness. Few of us want to be the agent of their frustration and disappointment and anger. And few of us want to deny ourselves the pleasure of gazing at our children's happy faces. But good parenting leaves us no choice: it demands that we use our loving authority to insist on what's right (not what pleases the kids), and to insist on what's appropriate (not what keeps them smiling). They themselves would rather be free of our restraint and authority, which is why they resist us, why they complain and whine and try to negotiate a better deal. Under such pressure, many of us cave—especially when we're committed to the happiness creed. (Despite their protests, there are times in their lives when children feel relieved and comforted by parental limit-setting. Limits establish a boundary that kids sense they need but are not yet able to set for themselves. We see this frequently with adolescents, who cannot resist, without a parent's firm limit-setting, the force of peer pressure to do what they know is wrong. Children, at any age, often feel overwhelmed by the power of their impulses, and appreciate, even if they don't show it, the role of parental limit-setting in bringing those impulses under control.)

> "...All their lives I have pushed myself to wit's end trying to keep them happy," says one mother, "allowing them to participate in sports when I know I can hardly get them to practice, letting them go out to movies with their friends when I know I can't afford it, letting them buy clothes that I know I don't approve of...just to keep them happy."

Many parents have been seduced by the appealing but dangerous notion of parent-as-friend. The generation gap that existed forty and fifty years ago has narrowed as parents have adopted youthful ways of dress, of lifestyle, of thinking. When "fifty is the new thirty," the line separating the generations is harder to find. One survey found that 44% of mothers thought "it's a good idea to treat your kids like friends."[26] It's an alarming statistic because friends don't discipline friends; friends don't set firm limits. If parents won't do it, who will?

> "Friendship with one's child can be a bright spot in an otherwise unhappy life. Enjoying a child's company is one of the main reasons that we have kids in the first place. But if we spoil our children with material goods in order to get a hug, or fail to set appropriate limits out of fear that they will withdraw their love or be upset, we have burdened them with protecting *us* from unhappiness."[27]

39

In the days before "Question Authority" became a popular bumper sticker, parents seemed more willing to lay down the law, to get tough when necessary. "This is for your own good," many of us remember our folks saying, and of course we couldn't understand at the time how a rule or a punishment or a restriction could be of any benefit. But it was the chores we were pressed to do, the curfew we were forced to keep, and the manners we were expected to adopt that helped us develop self-control, respect for others, and a sense of responsibility. It might never have happened had our parents been afraid to let us sometimes feel unhappy.

> Sean's parents were called to school to discuss his failing grades. He'd been a good student in the past, but was spending more and more time in front of the videogame screen, and less and less time on schoolwork. "I don't want to make a battle of getting him to do his homework," Sean's father said. "It's not worth it, stressing out at his age. We do a lot together, sports and games…we have a good time, and I'd hate to spoil it by coming down too hard on him."

It's not that uncommon, parents abdicating their proper role for the sake of short-term family harmony, while forgetting the long-term benefits that accrue from loving and caring discipline.

We overprotect our children from adversity

Wonder Bread, the slogan told us years ago, helps build strong bodies twelve ways. Adversity—the ordinary challenges of childhood—does the same for our emotional muscles. But many devotees of *I just want them to be happy* try to shield their children from all the varieties of life's pain, all the so-called negative feelings: hurt, sadness, upset, envy, etc. The result? Children whose emotional muscles are weak rather than hearty, who crumple rather than bounce back when life doesn't go their way. They're lacking resilience, these over-shielded kids, a quality that only develops through encounters with adversity early in life.

> "If we fail to learn in childhood how to handle the full catastrophe of a rich life, we grow up emotionally ill prepared. Learning to build these inner resources for a happier life demands that we endure the hard knocks of the playground—boot camp for the inevitable upsets of everyday relationships. Given how the brain masters social resilience, children need to rehearse for the ups and downs of social life, not experience a steady monotone of delight."[28]

Neuroscientists say that youngsters exposed to stress develop, through repeated exposures, patterns in their brain circuitry that strengthen their capacity to cope with future stresses. With loving guidance, kids can become skilled at bringing themselves back to a "normal" emotional state—the essence of resilience—after something has knocked them off kilter. Too much shielding by parents may keep a smile on a face today, but promises a frown tomorrow when life overwhelms the ill prepared.

> A mother sought counseling to discuss her 14-year-old son's difficulty getting along with a boy who lived at the end of the block. "Terrence is *so* unhappy," she said despairingly. She described how the other boy teases Terrence whenever they pass each other. When asked how she has handled the situation, she proudly detailed her telephone calls to the boy's parents, her public admonishments of the youngster when she encounters him in the park, and her insistence that Terrence report to her immediately whenever he is on the receiving end of a rude remark or menacing stare. She balked at the suggestion that she might let Terrence develop his own ways of handling the situation, without her direct involvement. "It makes him so unhappy sometimes," she said, "which really gets to me."

So many parents today define good parenting as protecting their kids from indignities and disappointments. This seems especially true in families with social and economic privilege, the upper-middle-class parents accustomed to living "the good life." Many freely open their coffers to their sons and daughters without regard for the fact that the kids haven't worked for that buck, probably don't yet appreciate "the value of a dollar." But it's part of keeping the kids happy, extending the parent's economic privilege to everyone in the nest.

"I have a lot of advantages in life," said one father, "after all the years of working hard, saving and investing and struggling to get where I'm at. If my kids have to work hard for everything, I end up feeling guilty about it—like, why should I have it so easy while they have it hard? Isn't it the right thing to do, sharing the wealth and the privileges? My parents helped me when they could, and that's all I'm trying to do for [my kids]."

Many parents assume that someday their children will enjoy an economic lifestyle comparable to or even beyond their own. But what about the fact that some offspring of well-to-do parents, by virtue of a changing economy or personal career choice, won't attain a similar standard of living to the one their parents have accustomed them to. Will those kids, as adults with reduced resources, be able to adjust? Not easily, if they've faced little to no adversity in their lives.

Picture the decisions and situations your child will be faced with once she leaves home, during college and in her twenties: entering the work world, dating, interacting with landlords and neighbors and so many others. You know of course that countless challenges, disappointments, and frustrations will come her way—as happens to all of us. Is the experience you're giving your daughter at home while she is young preparing her to cope effectively with setbacks? In her life with you, is she gaining the necessary practice she needs so that she'll know what to do when things don't go her way? Is she learning how to "manage" frustration and disappointment and upset?

It goes beyond economics, parents flexing their muscles on their kids' behalf, fending off every challenge to their youngsters' happiness. More and more we see parents on the lookout for anyone who seems to get in their children's way. Teachers, principals, and coaches, exercising their proper authority, are some of the most frequent targets of these parents' crusade:

> It was the third week of the new school year and eight-year-old Jason complained that he didn't like his teacher. During a meeting with the principal, the father turned to Jason and asked, "What don't you like?" "She's not as nice as Mrs. Y was last year," Jason said. "She won't smile." Whereupon the father turned to the principal and said, "I don't think the new teacher understands him very well, or he wouldn't feel this unhappy with her. Can you reassign him?"

When *I just want them to be happy* attains a critical mass of community endorsement, we see schools and scouts and athletic organizations deciding to forego winners and losers in traditional competitions. "All are winners," the new attitude declares, so that no child is asked to face the difficult feelings—disappointment, sadness, upset—when, as an individual or a member of a team, she doesn't come out on top. It's an approach that coddles our kids instead of preparing them for one of life's realities: we cannot be winners all the time.

A few words about our kids' feelings...

Let your kids feel their hurt or sadness or upset or anger without getting in the way. Don't immediately try to change it or fix it or solve it. Don't soothe their pain prematurely with food or play or other distractions. Instead, listen to their story, and if they haven't named their feelings, do it for them: "Sounds like you're hurt." "I can see how upset you are." "You're really angry with me."

After the feelings are named (labeled), validate them:

"Everyone is *sad* sometimes. It's okay to be sad. There are good reasons you feel that way."

"I know you're *angry* with me right now. It's okay to be angry. You don't have to like everything I do."

"You're *upset* that your team lost. It's natural to feel that way. Your teammates probably feel that way, too."

"I'd feel *disappointed*, just like you, if I came down with the flu and couldn't attend a party. Things don't always work out the way we'd like."

Do nothing to short-circuit your child's expression of emotional pain. Be careful not to hijack the moment—not to shut your child down—by criticizing or preaching or saying some version of, "I told you so." Teach your kids that one way feelings pass is by expressing them through words, written or spoken. (You can console and comfort, teach lessons and administer consequences later, after the feelings have been voiced.) It's only through enduring the tough moments of emotional pain that your kids build their emotional muscles.

Those of us who can't feel and accept our own emotional pain are going to have a hard time allowing our kids to feel theirs. In that case, we should seek professional guidance to learn how to handle painful feelings more effectively, if only for our kids' sake.

A father phoned during the final weeks of summer. His daughter was upset anticipating the start of high school because her closest friends had all been accepted at prestigious private schools. Her application had been turned down by those programs. She feared she'd be unable to make friends at her new school. She was crying a lot, which understandably caused her father much distress. He wondered if he should try to persuade one of the other schools to squeeze her in. We talked with him about ways to help his daughter understand and accept her difficult feelings, and reminded him that facing this adversity today will enable her to better face adversity tomorrow.

Perhaps your kids are doing great. Many over-shielded children are well-adjusted and successful, obedient and respectful. But don't be fooled into thinking that because they're doing well today, they will have the coping skills they'll need later, after they leave their sheltered nests. (Consider the increased incidence in recent years of adjustment problems among college freshmen. Are today's kids less well-prepared than generations past—too protected, too indulged—to cope with the challenges of being on their own?) If your child has been rather over-protected, ask yourself: How can I reduce the size of the safety net I've been providing, even if it means my child will come home with a bump or an emotional scrape now and then? Where can I step back and allow my son or daughter the practice of encountering a bit of adversity?

We emphasize feelings over actions

Society rises and falls not as a result of how people *feel*, but of how people *act*. Feelings can't be counted on to lead us to do the right thing, whether as members of a body politic, in our personal relationships, or as a parent. We all know how feelings can lead us to say or do what the logical, rational mind later regrets. That's because our emotions erupt quickly, often automatically, while reason moves at a slower pace. Scientists attribute this to the fact that the emotional part of the brain, which developed far earlier in neurological evolution, had to react quickly to protect our early ancestors from the multitude of dangers and threats to survival. Speed, coupled with evolutionary seniority, give the emotional brain a certain power and dominance over the "younger" portions of the brain, which regulate logic and reason.

That's why it makes no sense to elevate a feeling—happiness—above everything else. Our children need to learn that much of what brings about success in life, particularly success in relationships, comes not from how we feel, but from *what we do*.

Feeling happy offers no guarantee that a life is lived well or lived right. People have been known to be happy and cruel, happy and self-centered, happy and thoughtless. We have no reason to expect that a society of happy people would be good and just and fair, simply because happiness abounded. Perhaps Al Capone was happy. Or Stalin, or Hitler. Many abusive spouses we've counseled have told us they're happy. We read, too, about unethical politicians and dishonest CEOs whose friends and associates, interviewed outside the courtroom, describe the defendant as a happy person—happy and corrupt.

In review, when we only want our children to be happy, how easy it is to become entrapped by one or more of these five misguided consequences:

- We're captive to our children's moods.
- We feel unnecessary guilt and shame.
- We abdicate parental authority.
- We overprotect our children from adversity.
- We emphasize feelings over actions.

And yet, despite the reasons for parents to eschew the happiness creed, it remains true that happiness is a desirable, and inevitable, goal—something people have pursued from the beginning of time and probably always will. If giving voice and believing in *I just want them to be happy* is not the way to set our children on the path toward authentically happy lives, what is the way? A multitude of formulas abound—in literature, in religion, in popular culture, in family traditions. Is there a path that parents can set their children upon that is most likely to lead to authentic happiness? We will answer this question by looking first at three paths a great many families are traveling that may *not* get them where they want to go.

5

Three Happiness Myths

"A wealthy man is one who earns
$100 a year more than his wife's sister's husband."
H.L.Mencken

You say *I just want them to be happy*, but what do you do? Where do you put your time, money, and energy when it comes to your kids? How do you know that the seeds you have been planting will lead them to thriving, contented lives?

By understanding the happiness research—separating the myths from the realities—we can say that many families have been sowing the wrong seeds.

Myth #1: Money leads to happiness

Americans today have more money in their pockets than they did fifty years ago. Since World War II, inflation-adjusted income has almost tripled. The size of homes has nearly doubled; an unimaginable assortment of consumer options are within reach. Yet the happiness of Americans during this time frame hasn't changed. Between the 1950s and today, the percentage of people reporting that they are "very happy" has re-mained the same—about 32%.[29] Despite our nation having grown richer, despite more people having access to a dizzying array of goods and services, we are no happier. The old adage would seem right: money buys convenience, but it doesn't buy happiness.

Yet it's not as simple as that.

Studies also show that money can buy at least some measure of happiness when it lifts us out of poverty: people at the lowest socio-economic rung show the lowest level of hap-piness. But beyond poverty, additional money does not ap-preciably improve morale.[30]/[31] A 2004 *Time* magazine poll found that happiness increases with household incomes up to about $50,000, with little added benefit when incomes rise above that.[32] The research is sometimes inconsistent, however. A different survey found that happiness increased *all along the income scale*: 23% of people earning less than $20,000 reported being "very happy"—they were at the bottom of the happiness scale—compared with 50% of the group with income $150,000 and above—they were at the top. In that survey, happiness in-creased at *every* income jump.[33] But these findings aren't typi-cal. *Most research supports the time-honored conclusion that money fails to predict happiness.* "People who go to work in their over-alls and on the bus," one investigator wrote, "are just as happy, on the average, as those in suits who drive to work in their own Mercedes."[34]

So why are the wealthiest people, as a rule, no happier than those who earn a modest wage? Most experts say it's be-cause we *adapt* to our changing asset levels and keep shifting our expectations upward. What we have in the bank on Monday begins to seem inadequate by Friday; the only way to stay happy is to accumulate more. Observations of lottery winners support this view: a temporary surge of happiness and then a return to the way they felt before the big win.[35]/[36] It's human nature, this attribute of adaptability, causing most of us to seek more and more money in order to stay as happy as we were.

Another viewpoint says that our happiness isn't tied to how much money we have, but whether we believe we have more (or less) than the next person. Human nature is at play again here, the unfortunate tendency to compare ourselves to others. Even though the U.S. has grown richer in fifty years, overall happiness has remained the same because *everyone* appears to be ahead; when we look around, we seem no better off than the neighbors—the rising tide has lifted all boats. Japan is a good example of this: the wealth of the Japanese, a relatively poor country in 1960, increased four-fold by the late 1980s, yet the average happiness level was found to be no higher in 1987 than twenty years before.[37] It's a pattern observed across a great many countries.

> Challenge the Myth
> Teach your children to avoid comparing their lot with that of others. Set an example: refuse to keep up with the Joneses, and tell your kids why. Show no interest when the media flaunts the lifestyles of the rich and famous: let your children see you switch the channel from stories about

> celebrities' earnings, the size of their homes, their lavish vacations. Talk about how such stories stir discontent and provoke greed. As a family, strive to live by these words from the Talmud: "Who is rich? He that rejoices in his portion."

What those without money don't know (but a survey of the Forbes wealthiest 100 uncovered) is that wealth can increase or decrease happiness, depending on *how it's used* and *what it means* in the lives of its owners. Although 75% of the most wealthy Americans (household incomes of $150,000 or more) say that as they have amassed more money, they have become happier[38], researchers suspect that it's the work—challenging, stimulating, *meaningful*—and not the dollars that accounts for the reported happiness. Sixty-one percent of the wealthy said that working "provides me with a challenge I enjoy."

Some researchers theorize that when wealthier people are happier, it's because they use their assets to buy *experience*, not stuff.[39] It's not the fancier car, the bigger house, or the new wardrobe that accounts for the happiness of some people at the higher ends of the income scale, it's the family vacation, the hobbies and leisure time, and the gatherings with friends for dinners and good times. Pleasurable, rewarding experiences seem to boost life satisfaction in ways material consumption cannot.

But people don't appreciate the value of experience over stuff, which is one reason the consumption treadmill isn't slowing down. One writer noted that America is perhaps the only country that has elevated shopping to a national pastime, exceeding football, golf, and NASCAR combined in time and dollars spent. Consumerism remains one of the most powerful values we impart to our kids, reinforced from the time they're young, when TV (and now the Internet) expose them to a constant flow of commercial messages. (We might take a lesson from Sweden, which has banned TV advertising aimed at kids.) But there's more than advertising at play here. Consumerism is reinforced each time our children see us come home with yet another brimming shopping bag, and when we fill our leisure time as a family by walking through the mall. "It's just so easy to pile the kids in the car and head for the mall when there's nothing else to do," said one mother. "It's sort of a retail circus, always changing and always stimulating, with something for everyone."

Challenge the Myth
Teach your children to value experience more than stuff. Replace shopping as a family pastime with a trip to the zoo, bowling alley or tossing a ball in your neighborhood park. Go cycling together or take a drive in the country. Buy yourselves ice cream cones and explore a new neighborhood on foot. As a fam-

---

> ily, build a model car, home, or airplane together; assemble a puzzle. Preach to the kids that while we give ourselves material goods to create momentary pleasures and convenience, we don't expect to find real happiness through stuff.

Is there any likelihood that the allure and power of consumer spending can be curtailed? Research shows that children today are more motivated toward the accumulation of money than in decades past. A survey of college freshmen in 1970 found 39% motivated primarily by the acquisition of money; in 1998, the percentage had risen to 74%.[40] A 2006 survey found that nearly three-quarters of college students believe it is essential or very important to be financially well-off, compared with 62.5% in 1980 and 42% in 1966.[41] Another poll found that 80% of 18-25 year-olds see getting rich as a top life goal for their generation.[42] How much are we parents responsible for this trend? How fervently do we chase the dollar while our kids watch and learn? There's a reason *Rich Dad, Poor Dad* has been on the *New York Times* bestseller list for over 300 weeks: teaching our kids how to get and stay rich is one of our top priorities.

Nobody is helping our young people make the connection between a nation growing richer in recent decades and the increasing rates of depression, divorce, and suicide. One psychologist calls it the American paradox: "the conjunction of material prosperity and social recession."[43] We've shared this perspective with parents many times, telling them about studies showing that materialistic kids have lower grades and higher rates of depression and substance use than non-materialistic kids.[44] How do parents react when we share this information? They simply squirm.

Myth #2: Achievement leads to happiness

Why so much fuss over test scores and college choice? There's no evidence that people with high test scores or fancy alma maters are any happier than others. Not even career success has been associated with happiness. Interviews with traditionally successful people holding the jobs society regards as most prestigious—doctors, lawyers, CEOs—reveal that many compare themselves to others who they believe are even more successful, leaving them feeling less satisfied in the end. (There it is again, human nature making its ill-fated comparisons, throwing up roadblocks to happiness.)

In our work with middle- and upper-middle-class families, we regularly encounter parents overly focused on achievement, pushing kids beyond their actual abilities, hoping to motivate them toward higher and higher levels of accomplishment. And why? It's as though these parents are convinced that the happy life is reserved for those with exceptional talents or academic success. But it's just not so: the "average" child has the same likelihood of living a flourishing, contented life as the "exceptional" child. Yet parents refuse to believe it, sparking in the past ten to fifteen years an "outbreak of specialness": an unwillingness to accept the idea that any son or daughter is merely average.[45] Many parents insist on labeling their children as exceptional, and are quick to blame teachers and schools when the kids earn ordinary grades. An entire industry of after-school and weekend learning centers has sprung up, feeding on parents' inability to accept average sons or daughters.

> Challenge the Myth
> Emphasize the pleasures of learning over the importance of grades. Encourage your kids' curiosity about whatever engages their interest, even if there are no awards at the end of that road, no gold stars or AP credits. Don't buy into a narrow view of what's worthwhile simply because its pursuit might enhance a college application. A youngster might find joy in building a ham radio (rather than excelling at soccer), or collecting stamps and coins (rather than honing violin skills).

One unfortunate consequence of pushing children to deliver excellence is the pressure on average kids to be other than what they are. Teens in particular may feel little freedom to navigate adolescence as it was meant to be experienced: a time of self-discovery, a time to explore what interests them. It's no wonder that so many are anxious and depressed, even on rare occasions taking their own lives.[46] Nor is it any wonder that the incidence of academic cheating has been on the rise, according to some experts.[47]

> Challenge the Myth
> Teach your children that life isn't a competition, that every under-taking doesn't require us to do our best. It's another misguided mantra of parenting: "Always do your best." Sometimes it's won-derful to learn (and play) with-out pressure, without having to "perform" to some arbitrary standard of excellence. "Always do your best" makes it hard to learn the pleasure of "taking it easy." In life, does every drawing need to be a masterpiece, every golf game a personal best?

Wendy Mogul, in *The Blessing of a Skinned Knee*, writes about parents who see their children's achievement as an im-portant family "product," a reflection of the family's status or worth, like driving a fancy car or installing the trendiest kitchen. "This attitude leads to an upside-down, child-centered perspective where we cater to children's whims yet pressure them to achieve at all costs—academically, socially, athleti-cally."[48]

Parents' obsession with achievement shows up in many ways. Even before kids are old enough to ride a bike, parents scramble for a spot in the "right" pre-schools. Their belief is that the path to success—and happiness—can never begin too soon. Educational toys and games cater to this market, promising to give youngsters a head start on all sorts of learning-related skills. And parents fill their kids' after-school and weekend schedules with enrichment lessons and classes and activities, believing that the more interests and talents and skills a child develops, the better positioned she is for success (and happiness) later on. These parents don't know that in over-scheduling their children, they sacrifice the time children need for *one of the most critical building blocks for a happy life*: free, unstructured play. (We discuss play at length in Chapter 16.)

What about work and career? Has the happiness research turned up evidence that members of any one profession or trade are happier than members of any other? No! When it comes to contentment, what matters is being employed in a way that uses one's strengths or talents. There's no evidence that doctors, lawyers and movie stars are happier than bakers, bus drivers, and mid-level managers. And yet, many of us pressure our sons and daughters toward certain fields of endeavor, as if those fields—especially the prestigious ones—assure a thriving, contented life.

Myth #3: Options lead to happiness

Sylvie, an eighth-grader in private school, was accepted to four of the six high schools she had applied to for the following fall. "I'm disappointed and shocked at the acceptances," Sylvie's mother said. "Four schools does-n't offer my daughter enough of a choice. I don't want her to end up unhappy."

Many of us seem convinced that our children's well-being depends on them having a multitude of options in their lives. Choices—lots and lots of choices. A kind of tyranny of personal choice has set in, fueled largely by a consumer mar-ketplace constantly trotting out new products and services, and promoting the notion that there's always one best and perfect choice for me.

Research doesn't support the importance of options as a predictor of happiness. On the contrary, studies have found that too much choice leads to less satisfaction, not more. For young children, confusion and anxiety can set in when an array of options are offered. Too many choices encourage us to doubt the value of what we've chosen, to second-guess ourselves by imagining that the road not taken might have been the road preferred. That's the problem with so much choice: human na-ture comparing again, imagining that the grass is greener. Re-search shows that people with fewer options generally feel more satisfied with the choices they make.[49]

In sum, what studies tell us is what philosophers, schol-ars, and wise people have known all along: *external circum-stances rarely predict authentic happiness.* People whose lives seem relatively easy are often unhappy, while many whose lives seem relatively rough are often content. Some of the poor are happy, many of the rich are not. (In an international survey, Nigeria ranks as the country whose people are the happiest.[50]) Low achievers are often happy, high achievers not. Good and bad events *do* influence our mood, but the effect appears to be temporary and we tend to revert to the level of happiness we knew before.[51]

So much of what we know about happiness comes as the result of a shift that occurred in psychology toward the end of the twentieth century, a shift that recognized the importance of understanding human flourishing and not just human suffering. When, in 1998, psychologist Martin Seligman, then the president of the American Psychological Association, declared that the time was right to study and promote all the ways things can go right in human development, he officially elevated happiness to a respectable topic of scientific inquiry. The pace of happiness research has picked up since then; investigators have been talking to people all across the globe, trying to understand how much our well-being derives from genes (nature), and how much from upbringing (nurture); how much from our thoughts, decisions, and actions, and how much from the random twists of fate that visit fortune and good health onto some more than others. Is it possible to increase our level of happiness—things we can do, attitudes we can hold, habits we can cultivate? If money and achievement and options don't predict happiness, what does? We turn now to that big question.

PART TWO

PLANTING THE SEEDS
OF AUTHENTIC HAPPINESS

6

Is There a Genetic Advantage?

"Happiness depends, as Nature shows,
Less on exterior things than most suppose."
William Cowper

Many psychologists talk about the genetic advantage. Who doesn't have an aunt or uncle, friend or neighbor, who was an anxious and fearful child, and still, as an adult, tends to be a not-very-happy worrier? Or a relative who was cheerful in her toddler years and remains sunny and optimistic today? Some of the differences among people have long been regarded as a function of inborn temperament, the genetic endowment that accompanies us into the world. Qualities of temperament seem to show up early. Parents report, and research corroborates, that even with twins, one can be happy while the other is grim; one can be knocked off kilter easily while the other rolls with the punches. Observations like these have become the basis for the *setpoint theory*: despite fluctuations in the face of life's ups and downs, all of us revert to some level of happiness dictated by temperament and personality. Say, for instance, we suffer an arm injury and are forced to abandon a favorite sport. Our despair tends to be temporary and then we're back to the level of happiness we felt before. A fair amount of research supports the setpoint theory. A seventeen-year study of German men and women found that only a quarter of the sample reported significant fluctuations in their level of life satisfaction *over time*. Three-quarters of the participants remained consistently happy (or unhappy) despite changing events and circumstances in their lives.[52]

But more recent thinking, coming out of the field of neuroscience, challenges the long-held view that temperament is fixed at birth. While it is true that we come into the world with a certain genetic portfolio, increasing evidence suggests that a child's interactions with the environment—the primary caregivers and the peer group, most of all—influence the ultimate expression of those genes.

> "It is biologically impossible for a gene to operate independently of its environment. Genes are designed to be regulated by signals from their immediate surround, including hormones from the endocrine system and neurotransmitters in the brain—some of which, in turn, are profoundly influenced by our social interactions." [53]

We can imagine, then, that a child born with a genetic propensity towards fearfulness might, under certain conditions—say, highly optimistic parents plus stable and reliable nurturing—develop into a hearty and resilient person, someone for whom fear does not color her life. That same child, exposed to a different set of circumstances, might very well have turned out fearful and avoidant. Depending on the environment, the genetic propensity can aim in different directions. "Like a plant adapting to rich or to depleted soil, a child's brain shapes itself to fit its social ecology, particularly the emotional climate fostered by the main people in her life."[54]

Science has only recently come to understand the way the brain changes itself in response to experience. The notion of an unchanging temperament from birth no longer holds up. Genetics, then, is influential, but it does not *fix* the odds on our building contented lives. Parents command great power—the seeds they plant, the soil they till—to tip the genetic scales in one direction or another. From our review of decades of happiness research, we have distilled out eight key ingredients that best predict contented, thriving lives. These are the seeds for a parent to plant, the seeds that can grow into authentic happiness:

- Good mental and physical health
- A life of meaning
- Closeness to others
- Acts of loving kindness
- A sense of gratitude
- A sense of spirituality
- An optimistic outlook
- Gratifying pursuits

Let's examine each seed in turn.

7

Teach the Habits of Good Health

"Health is not valued till sickness comes."
Dr. Thomas Fuller

It isn't exactly good health that predicts happiness. Researchers say we take good health for granted—don't think about it, don't take delight in it. It's *bad* health that's the problem—chronic illness or disability. They are hard to ignore, and have been found to reduce levels of happiness.

And mental illness reduces happiness most of all.[55]

In one study, 55% of people who said their health was poor also said they were "not too happy."[56] Of course, not everyone with poor health is subject to a life of despair, as we know from stories of people who lead rich and fulfilling lives despite an affliction. But they may be the exception. That's why helping children develop *habits* and *attitudes* that promote good health (and safety) is a way parents can plant a seed toward lifelong happiness.

Part of the challenge of chronic illness or disability is how it reduces for many people a sense of control in their day-to-day lives. "Being effective—changing things, influencing things, making things happen—is one of the fundamental

needs with which human brains seem to be naturally en-
dowed."[57] Research suggests that when people lose or are
much reduced in their ability to control things—being confined
to a wheelchair or crippled with severe arthritis—they are at
higher risk for unhappiness and depression.[58]

> Plant a Seed
> Teach your children, by words
> and example, to value good
> health and the habits that pro-
> mote it: moderation and balance
> in work and play, healthful eat-
> ing, regular exercise, adequate
> sleep, and the avoidance of ciga-
> rettes and excessive alcohol.

Taking responsibility for one's good health is an attitude that parents can model for their children: let them see that
you don't neglect problems that arise, and that you educate
yourself around all aspects of your (and their) medical care. Encourage your kids to ask questions of their doctors, and, when
they are old enough, to understand the causes of ordinary
health conditions—colds and flu, muscle and stomach
aches—as well as the reasons we treat those conditions the way
we do. Help them understand the concept of stress, our body's
need for sleep, and the importance of relaxation as a counter-
balance to busy, active lives.

Certain forms of mental illness can interfere profoundly
with happiness. One study found that clinical depression, even
more than poverty, contributed significantly to unhappiness.[59]

"Mental illness is probably the largest single cause of misery in Western societies."[60] Like chronic illness or disability, mental illness creates a *lasting* reduction in happiness, not just a temporary dip until we return to our setpoint.

What can we do to minimize the likelihood of severe psychological problems in our children? Providing them with a solid foundation of connectedness, which we discuss at length in Chapter 15, may be the best inoculation we can give them against severe mental illness. Equally important, and often overlooked, is taking care of our own mental health. Make every family member's emotional well-being—this includes your own!—an acceptable topic around the dinner table. Break the taboo of past generations and speak openly about anxiety and stress, sadness and grief, etc.

Plant a Seed

Let your children hear you talk about challenging feelings and difficult moods: "I've been feeling sad lately, ever since Grandma died," or "All day long I've been upset about the damage I did to the car yesterday," or "I've been pretty grumpy lately, maybe because I haven't been sleeping well at night." And let them hear you describe the constructive ways you are handling those feelings.

> "I've been talking to people at work about Grandma's death, and it seems to help me feel better," or "I know my upset will pass, as it always does," or "I'll phone my doctor and see if I can get some help with that sleep problem."

We don't always recognize when our psychological health is impaired. It's common to "fool ourselves" into denying problems and conditions we might not want to see. If we have any reason to wonder how we're doing emotionally, it may help to ask trusted others—a spouse or close friend—what *they* notice about our habits and moods and idiosyncrasies. You can say, "Do I seem okay to you? I'm wondering if I'm depressed lately?" Or, "Do my moods seem balanced and even?" Or, "Do any of my habits sometimes seem odd or extreme?" Ask the right people in your life—people with good judgment and clear thinking—to really level with you about what they see, and promise not to "shoot the messenger" if they offer observations that make you uncomfortable. (Remind yourself that if such feedback ultimately helps your children—and it can!—then it's worth hearing.)

Alternatively, make an appointment for a mental health check-up with a counselor or therapist if you've been in poor emotional shape for some time. (Again, it's common for people not to recognize psychological problems in themselves; the mind often doesn't want to see it, doesn't want to confront a difficult reality.) Our children need us to be the emotionally healthiest we can be, which is why we should seek help when we need it. Casually, while slicing the vegetables or folding the laundry, let your children know you've met with a counselor or therapist—this teaches them that there is nothing shameful in seeking professional help—just as you might speak about a visit to the dentist or the dermatologist.

It comes as no surprise that studies have found higher incidences of psychiatric problems in the offspring of parents with significant emotional troubles of their own. When our own psychological health and emotional well-being is compromised, it's hard for us to give our children what they need to set them on the road toward a happy life.

8

Promote a Life of Meaning

*"The only true happiness comes from squandering
ourselves for a purpose."*
William Cowper

Happy, flourishing people have created a sense of meaning in their lives, a purpose in living that anchors them to something beyond their own fleeting pleasures and gratifications. One study found that seven in ten individuals without a clearly defined purpose felt unsettled about their lives, while almost seven in ten with a purpose felt satisfied.[61]

Sometimes meaning comes from work, sometimes from community: volunteer service, politics, neighborhood projects. For many, meaning comes from raising kids and supporting a family. "Since I've had children," writes psychiatrist Hallowell, "I've gained purpose and direction, worked harder than ever, and gotten more done than I ever have before. This is because I have a reason greater than myself to go out and provide."[62]

We must teach our children that meaning is found *outside ourselves*, not in an attachment to our own needs and wants and feelings. Neither does meaning come from the pursuit of *pleasures,* the fleeting gratifications which leave little trace afterwards. True meaning comes from activities whose payoffs linger in our hearts and minds. It could be a spiritual practice, a commitment to a worthy cause, a dedication to art or music or beauty. Any line of work can offer a sense of meaning, and when work cannot provide more than a salary that's needed for food and shelter, meaning can come from other places, from involvements and pursuits outside the daily grind. We know a man who walks up and down the beach several times a week, removing litter and debris. He says he feels good doing something for the environment, and knowing how much pleasure others derive from his efforts. An amateur dog breeder talks about the joy she feels knowing her animals give so much pleasure to others.

> Plant a Seed
> Talk with your children about the importance of living life with a sense of purpose. Share with them the sources of meaning in your own life, and invite friends and family, when the kids are around, to talk about their own sources of meaning. Ask your kids who they admire in the world, and why. Tell them whom you have admired, and talk about the people who have been cultural heroes in the past.

Nowadays, popular heroes earn their status through surface qualities—looks and talents—rather than aspects of character and virtue that captivated the youth of earlier generations. From the outside, it's hard to see a sense of meaning in the lives of so many "stars" in our celebrity culture, where fame is elevated for its own sake, *devoid of content*. Business and political figures no longer invite the easy admiration they might have enjoyed in the past. "To the extent that young people now find it hard to take seriously their relationship with God," writes psychologist Seligman, "to care about their relationship with the country, or to be part of a large and abiding family, they will find it very difficult to find meaning in life."[63]

Plant a Seed

Help your children feel part of something larger than themselves, a chain of humanity. And help them understand that all of us stand on the shoulders of those who came before us, who made a difference through their own meaningful lives. Keep meaningful mementos and photographs of ancestors around the house; create a family tree. Visit the gravesites of family members and talk about the values dear to them, what they stood for. Educate your kids about the influen-

---

> tial leaders and visionaries in
> your particular ethnic, racial, or
> religious group.

Our kids need heroes, people whose lives reflect core values and principles—real meaning—and whose lives represent more than a fleeting fad. It's natural for children, especially at the youngest ages, to look to their parents to be their heroes. Are we up to the task? Do the lives we lead and the values we teach carry a sense of *meaning*—lessons we're proud to pass on to them and, through them, to generations beyond? There's little true and lasting meaning in what our kids witness in the consumer culture: miles of malls and product advertisements and endless cycles of shopping. We're in competition with the popular culture for our kids' often-limited attention: our own messages of meaning versus the empty materialism all around them.

Is it a fight we're determined to win?

9

Encourage Closeness

*"When we seek for connection, we restore the world
to wholeness. Our seemingly separate lives become
meaningful as we discover how truly necessary we
are to each other."*

Margaret Wheatley

We're social animals, we *homo sapiens*. Evolutionary psychologists and biologists tell us we're hard-wired that way: social bonds played an important role in early survival. Thousands of years ago, membership in a clan contributed to the successful rearing of the young, assured survival through the sharing of food and water, and offered better defense against enemies and forces of nature. Back then, nobody could have done it alone.

Research provides strong evidence for the crucial place of human connection in happy lives. People with close relationships have been found to be more contented and in better health.[64]

"The most striking finding on relationships and physical health is that socially integrated people—those who are married, have close family and friends, belong to social and religious groups, and participate widely in these networks—recover more quickly from disease and live longer. Roughly eighteen studies show a strong connection between social connectivity and mortality."[65]

A study at the University of Illinois found that the students reporting the highest levels of happiness (and the least depression) had the strongest ties to friends and family.[66] Loneliness has been found to correlate with poorer immune and cardio-vascular function.[67]

> Plant a Seed
> Teach the value of friendship by welcoming your kids' friends into your home. Encourage sleepovers. When possible, include their friends in your family outings and vacations. Do more than just take the friends along: show interest in their lives and in their families, and share of yourself with them. Open your home to your own friends and family, so your kids can see you valuing your own connections.

There's a chicken and egg question here: do happier people reach out more to others and build connections, or do connections shape happier people? We believe it works both ways. But it's no great leap to imagine that even the least happy person enjoys a bit of a boost when there's someone to talk to, if only occasionally.

Beyond the important connection with parents, (which we discuss at length in Chapter 15), children learn the ins and outs of building closeness as soon as they're able to play with siblings and friends. As they get older, talk to them about *how* to find the right friends, people who share their interests and their values. Be careful not to pressure your children into social groups that are wrong for them, perhaps because of your own latent wishes—unfulfilled when you were young—to be part of the "popular crowd" or the "artsy crowd." Consider who your children are—not who you want them to be—when you create social opportunities for them: selecting a summer camp or enrolling them in after-school classes or activities.

Overscheduled children sometimes are so busy with homework and lessons and extra-curricular activities that the opportunities for them to enjoy casual connections are reduced. Parents must remember the value for kids in just sitting around with friends, chatting and laughing and developing relationship skills.

Teach your kids that the quality of friendships matters more than the quantity; friendships with less conflict and more mutuality—shared interests, reciprocal caring, empathy, good communication skills—contribute to greater happiness and health than friendships rife with tension.[68] One study found that a tone of ongoing criticalness in a relationship reduced people's happiness by about one-third.[69] Neuroscience research points to a connection between distressing relationships and elevated levels of stress hormones which can damage certain genes that control virus-fighting cells.[70] "Toxic" and unhappy relationships have also been associated, in studies, with negative effects on blood pressure and cardiovascular health. It makes sense, then, to help your kids develop relationship skills. Teach them that conflict is a part of all relationships and can usually be resolved through patient listening and calm communication. Practice with them the skill of perspective-taking: imagining how the world might look through another person's eyes.

Plant a Seed

Are you comfortable having the kids around, listening and watching while you and your spouse or partner argue or disagree? If not, it may be a sign that you're not proud of your conflict-resolution skills. Many of us aren't. If your skills need improvement, take a class or workshop, or schedule several sessions with a counselor. Your kids need to learn from you— who else will teach them?—how to disagree respectfully and fairly; they need to see that conflict, effectively dealt with, brings people closer in the end. The skills they pick up by watching (and imitating) you will impact their lives forever.

Perhaps the most common way people seek close connection is through marriage. Is there a relationship between
marriage and happiness? For a long time, popular wisdom
taught that married people are happier than unmarried people,
a viewpoint supported by a mountain of research. One recent
survey found that 43% of married people reported being "very
happy," compared to 24% of unmarried people.[71] Why might
this be? Perhaps it's some of marriage's benefits: a reduction in
loneliness, added security and companionship, a socially-ap-
proved and supported identity. More recent thinking says it
may not be marriage per se which produces the happiness effect, but the fact of living in close connection to someone. *Attachment* versus *isolation*. That's why some investigators say that
single people with strong connections and close friendships
may be just as happy as married people.

A few words about empathy...

For stronger friendships, more satisfying marriages, and happier children, practice empathy.
    Empathy is the ability to put ourselves in others' shoes
and imagine—even feel—what they're feeling, how they're ex-
periencing the world emotionally. Some researchers believe
that the capacity for empathy is evident from birth, that it may
be biologically wired within us. An example of this is "reflex-
ive crying," the way newborns cry when they hear other babies
wailing (but not when they hear their own crying on tape).
Neuroscience has identified "mirror neurons," perhaps the
brain's core agent of empathy. Mirror neurons cause people to
feel the emotions of others almost instantaneously, just by ob-

serving the expression on someone's face or hearing "feeling" tones in someone's voice. If our capacity for empathy is indeed present from birth, then it's within parents' power to either thwart that capacity or help it develop. Which category of parent are you?

Empathy begets empathy: parents who offer it are parents who promote it. "Look how *happy* you are!" "You're *frustrated* that the blocks keep falling." "The way you're sitting there, I sense that you're *sad*." "You're *excited* when we visit Grandma." Certainly it's hard to offer our kids empathy when they're pushing our buttons, when we're frustrated with them or angry. But that's when our empathy is particularly effective. When something is troubling our kids, or they've broken an agreement or fallen down on an expectation, pause before indulging the common tendency to correct and reprimand. *Think and listen first.* If you need more information to understand what's going on, ask *neutral* questions, without a critical tone of voice. "How did you come to that decision?" "What were you feeling at the time?" "Tell me all about it." "How do you feel now?"

Then, after they've expressed themselves, offer empathy:

"I see how *upset* you are."

"You're really *sad* about what happened."

"I sense you're *afraid* of my reaction."

"You were *confused* and didn't know what to do."

"You're *angry* at me for not giving you what you want."

If your empathy misses the mark, your child will probably tell you (or show you through her facial expression). You can try again: "Oh, I see, you're feeling..." You'll know when your empathy hits home by the nod of agreement or the look on your child's face that says, "Dad, you understand." After that, and only after that, should you offer your own thoughts: your advice or critique, as well as *your* feelings.

Empathy doesn't mean you abdicate your role as a teacher or a disciplinarian. It doesn't mean you forget to administer consequences or a reproving speech when that's what's needed. It just means you *strike a balance between emotional ally and moral guidepost.* Your children need both voices from you.

Here is an example of empathy in action:

Lin had turned 16 only two weeks ago and couldn't wait to take her driver's license exam. As expected, she passed the test and now looked forward to using the family car. Her mother thought Lin needed more practice parking, especially in the tight spaces along crowded city streets. But Lin was impatient and harassed her mother, who gave in—she just wants Lin to be happy—and allowed her to use the car one evening after school. As it turned out, Lin scraped the passenger door that night. When she returned home, her mother saw an expression of upset and fear.

"It looks like something's wrong," said Mother. (An empathic remark). Lin proceeded to describe what had happened.

"You must be very upset," Mother said. (Another empathic remark).

Lin nodded; her eyes became tearful.

"I know how horrible this must feel," Mother continued. "Something like this happened to me when I was a teenager." (More empathy, demonstrating a lot of sensitivity to Lin's feelings.)

With each empathic remark, Lin visibly relaxed. As she relaxed, she opened up and shared more of what happened to her, and how awful she felt. That's the power of empathy: it promotes a feeling of safety, which makes it easier for kids—for anyone—to open up. In time, after Lin's story was complete, Mother moved the conversation to the next step: what are they going to do about it? Will there be consequences? Will Lin be asked to pay for the repairs? A challenging situation, but at that point Lin felt that her mother was her ally, which was a good and important thing for both of them. With her mother's support, Lin made a plan to take responsibility for the damage.

10

Value Loving Kindness

*"That best portion of a good man's life,
His little, nameless, unremembered acts of
kindness and of love."*
William Wordsworth

Studies tell us that a high percentage of happy people engage in virtuous acts of loving kindness. It's not a new idea: all the world's great wisdom traditions teach that the way to find happiness is to give happiness. But it's a theme rarely heard outside those traditions nowadays, drowned out by a popular culture that encourages us to make our lives "all about me."

Research has shown that any form of service to others increases happiness. Studies have found that volunteer work in general, and performing five particular acts of kindness on a weekly basis, both significantly enhanced life satisfaction.[72]/[73]/[74] One study found that people engaged in volunteer work are twice as likely to feel happy with themselves as non-volunteers.[75] Could it be that by giving to others, we feel good about ourselves—and happier with life? Could it be that acts of kindness contribute to the sense of meaning we discussed earlier, allowing us to believe that our own lives can make a difference?

> **Plant a Seed**
> Children are never too young to participate in acts of loving kindness. Turn birthdays and holidays into times for giving, not just receiving. Help your kids deliver the toys they've outgrown to a day care center or children's hospital—don't just do it for them. Volunteer together at a food pantry or animal shelter. Kids can practice loving kindness through the compassionate care of an animal and through babysitting younger children.

Professionals in the helping fields—social work, psychology, education—have told us that children of affluent backgrounds seem less generous and less altruistic than kids from other backgrounds. This should be a warning sign to parents: when a child's life is too easy, or when she receives too much too soon, she may have less inclination or capacity to engage in acts of loving kindness. That, in turn, may be a very real obstacle to her own later life happiness.

There's surprising new evidence to suggest that we're hardwired to take pleasure from helping, from acts of cooperation or kindness. One remarkable study found that when people behaved cooperatively during a laboratory experiment, their brains showed signs of pleasurable arousal, the same sort of arousal observed during a drug-induced high.[76] From the point of view of evolution, this isn't surprising: survival depended, thousands of years ago, on the ability to *share* resources and *cooperate* in mutual defense.

Plant a Seed

Be sure your children know about and witness your own acts of loving kindness. Talk with them about the charities you support, and ask for suggestions from them about worthy causes. Make a point of telling them when you've looked in on a suffering neighbor or family member, and enlist their help—chopping the onions, adding the chocolate chips—when you make a pot of soup or a batch of cookies for a sick friend.

Two hundred and fifty years ago, the philosopher Jeremy Bentham recognized the pay-off we're talking about here:

"Create all the happiness you are able to create: remove all the misery you are able to remove. Every day will allow you to add something to the pleasure of others, or to diminish something of their pains. And for every grain of enjoyment you sow in the bosom of another, you shall find a harvest in your own bosom; while every sorrow which you pluck out from the thoughts and feelings of a fellow creature shall be replaced by beautiful peace and joy in the sanctuary of your soul."[77]

11

Impart Gratitude

"Gratitude is the memory of the heart."
Italian proverb

It used to be easier to have gratitude. Before technology connected us so completely with everyone else—first through television, now through the Internet—we had little exposure to how others lived, to the material abundance of so many. Nowadays it's an assault. Widely-circulated *Parade* magazine each year publishes its "salary issue." On the cover is a gallery of diverse faces paired with their annual incomes. Several of the rich and famous are always included, smiling above their seven-digit salaries. On the Internet, AOL frequently posts articles about the nation's grandest homes or the most expensive automobiles. Television shows feature the "exclusive" resorts where celebrities vacation, the tony boutiques where they shop. The smiling images of these celebrities seem to shout, "I'm so happy!"

Even for the economically comfortable among us, it's easy to find our own share lacking when compared to the sheer abundance of the top one percent. How much tougher it is for individuals and families just scraping by.

The happiest people are those who cultivate a sense of gratitude, an attitude of appreciation for what they have—large or small. They are the people who have learned not to dwell on comparisons between what they have and the bounty of some others. "Success is getting what you want," said Dale Carnegie. "Happiness is wanting what you get."

Gratitude research has yielded some astonishing results. Studies have found that when people regularly recorded in a personal journal the things they felt grateful for, not only were they happier, but they took better care of their health.[78] Seligman's studies of gratitude found that when people wrote a personal testimonial to someone who positively influenced their lives, and then read the testimonial aloud to that person—the "gratitude visit"—they experienced a sense of increased life satisfaction *for up to three months*. He achieved an even longer-lasting effect—six months of increased satisfaction—when he asked people to write *on a daily basis* about "three blessings" that came their way: what went well and why.[79]

> Plant a Seed
> Model gratitude for your children by commenting frequently on the blessings in your life, especially during the tougher, challenging times when we tend to focus on the negative. Create a mealtime ritual, weekly or nightly, where each family member names one or two things that went well that day, one or two

things for which they are grateful. Children as young as three or four can be taught to participate in this activity. Bedtime, too, can include a ritual in which parent and child together review the events of the day and acknowledge what there is to be thankful for. "What went well today?"

We've all seen the excitement in a youngster who receives a new toy, plays with it for awhile and soon becomes bored. What seemed like happiness was merely a fleeting pleasure. Whatever gratitude he or she may have felt lasted until the toy's novelty wore off. That's why we have to teach our children to appreciate blessings that aren't so fleeting:

• Good health ("Remember when you were in bed with the flu? Let's take a moment and notice how wonderful it is to feel good again.")

• Good friends ("Remember how bored you felt last summer when your friends were away? Let's take a moment and notice how wonderful it feels to have your friends around.")

• Abundance ("Aren't we lucky that we have food to eat and clothes to wear?")

• All the other *non-material* blessings of their lives ("Aren't we lucky to have a pet? A brother or sister to play with? Friends and family who love you? Teachers who care about you?")

Gratitude can develop when children engage in acts of loving kindness that call attention to the ways they themselves are blessed or skilled or fortunate: mentoring or tutoring younger students, loaning a favorite toy to a sick friend, baking a cake as a welcome gift for new neighbors. One family we know, parents and kids together, assembles "goody bags" of fruit and chips, which they distribute on New Year's Day to the squatters in a homeless encampment at the center of their town. Even bringing into the world something of value to share— tending a garden of flowers or vegetables—can foster in children the feeling of gratitude for the abundance in their own lives as they deliver a bouquet or fruit basket to the housebound senior down the block.

Some children's books teach the value of gratitude: *It Could Always Be Worse*, by Margot Zemack, and *I Like Your Buttons*, by Sarah M. Lamstein. A knowledgeable librarian can help you find others.

And be careful of the expectations your children develop—they can serve as an obstacle to gratitude, and by extension a barrier to happiness. Dennis Prager writes that we're less grateful for things we expect and more grateful for life's surprises.[80] Hence one of the dangers in giving our children too much: they develop an expectation that life always provides, and so they feel less gratitude for the blessings that come their way. Mihaly Csikszentmihalyi observed that "children from the most affluent families...tend to be more bored, less involved, less enthusiastic, less excited."[81]

> Plant a Seed
> Gently denying our children some of the things they ask for is more likely to foster gratitude, than giving them so much that they come to expect that life's bounty is limitless. Even if you're inclined to give yourself, materially, most of the things you want does not mean you should do the same for your kids.

The consumer marketplace has fanned the flames of discontent in recent years by telling us that we should accept only "the best": the best restaurants, the best athletic shoes, the best hair salon, the best pediatrician. Nothing, this philosophy instructs, should be ordinary in our lives. The implication is that unless something is the best, it's not worth having—certainly not worth feeling grateful for. How easy, then, to become discontented with the ordinary: our "ordinary" marriages, our "ordinary" friends, our "ordinary" home, and our "ordinary" children. It's an attitude that has come to influence many of us into pressuring our kids—directly and indirectly—to be the best in every way: successful and beautiful and affectionate and talented.

> "My cousin Jake is this awesome athlete," lamented 16-year-old Mitchell, a member of his high school swim team. "My Dad always talks about how great Jake is, and if I tried harder and practiced more, I could be like Jake. I know I'll never be as good as he is. Sometimes I feel like quitting."

Caught up in our workaholic strivings for money and status—how grateful can we be if we have to keep striving?—many of us transmit those strivings to our children, the belief that more is better, that more is necessary. For the sake of our kids' happiness, we might be better off rethinking our approach and practicing gratitude for the blessings life has given us. The example we set will make a difference in our sons' and daughters' ability to feel gratitude in their own lives.

12

Imbue Spirituality

"The foundations of a person are not in matter but in spirit."
Ralph Waldo Emerson

oncern with the heart and the soul rather than the material world—that's the essence of spirituality. Research shows that spirituality is frequently an element in the lives of happy people. Those scoring highest on a scale of spiritual commitment in a 1984 survey were twice as likely to declare themselves "very happy" as compared to those lowest in spiritual commitment.[82]

For many families, organized religion provides the way; others seek it elsewhere, knowing that spirituality needs no pulpit, no church or mosque or temple, no membership dues. Feeling a connection to the deep places of the heart and soul, to the universe *beyond ourselves*, is possible in so many ways: through loving friendship and community, art and music, acts of kindness, meditation, the twelve step program—so long as we draw from and touch the deepest positive parts of ourselves, never the "scheming ego."[83]

> Plant a Seed
> Model spirituality for your chil-
> dren by demonstrating—not just
> saying—that you value heart
> and soul—in them, in yourself,
> in friends and family. Talk ad-
> miringly about love, forgiveness,
> respect, kindness and compas-
> sion wherever you find it.

Naturally curious, children wonder about some of the things we're often uncomfortable explaining and aren't so clear about for ourselves. "Why do people die?" "What makes people do bad things?" "Where did Grandpa go when he passed away?" "How come there's sickness?" Talking with your children about these and other "deep" questions, questions about the nature of life and the universe, allows a spiritual life to take root. When topics likes these come up, offer your opinions, or say, "I'm not sure." You don't need answers, but be open to the questions and glad to receive them. Delight in the process of exploring ideas that are beyond our certain knowledge, even though you may feel on shaky ground. Most of all, be open to your children's voices, to the answers that come from their own imaginations. "You may disagree with their answers," writes psychiatrist Hallowell, "but *what* they conclude is so much less important than *that* they conclude, that they delve into the un-known with curiosity and energy."[84]

Plant a Seed
Regardless of whether your children raise the questions, you can do so yourself, casually, around the dinner table: questions about the invisible world, about birth and death and good and evil. Draw the kids out; find out how their minds tackle these ideas. Conversations like these promote the development of a spiritual life.

As vehicles connecting us to the deeper places of heart and soul, rituals can be an important precursor to a child's developing sense of spirituality. That's why throughout all recorded time, ritual has held a central place in cultures and societies, fulfilling a spiritual need that seems fundamental to our species. At birthday celebrations, remember to acknowledge the preciousness of life and the miracle of birth; don't just offer gifts and a chocolate layer cake, but say something about the day's deeper meaning. At anniversary celebrations, acknowledge the joys of connection, commitment and trust. Milestone rituals—communions, bar mitzvahs, funerals—mark the passage of time, moments to reflect on deeper meanings: on being alive, on our connection to ancestors, on our hopes for the future. Other special days (holidays) offer opportunities to be grateful—for harvests, for cycles and rebirths, for the defeat of evil by goodness. Remember always to talk about these deeper meanings, and to draw the kids into the dialogue. ("What does this day mean to you?")

> **Plant a Seed**
>
> See that your family calendar includes a variety of rituals—weekly, monthly, annually—and use those moments to talk about the deeper meaning behind the day. Include plenty of sensory elements that children find so appealing—foods, colors, lights, sounds—and that will create warm and powerful memories to last a lifetime. Your kids' participation in richly meaningful rituals will promote a joyful place of spirituality in their lives.

In the pursuit of spirituality, organized religion has the advantage of a program already in place: ritual, community, teachings—you need only show up and join in. But don't expect infrequent and passive participation in prayer services several times a year to impart spirituality to your kids. It takes more than that; it takes weaving spirituality into your family life on a regular basis.

Studies in different nations have found that religiously involved people report higher levels of happiness than non-religious.[85] Religiously active widows, for instance, report more joy in their lives than widows without religious affiliation. And religiously active people seem to bounce back to happiness more easily after the upheaval of divorce, unemployment, and illness.[86]/[87] A study of third-year college students found that those who participated in religious activities were more likely to feel good about themselves and the direction they were headed, while a study of 12th graders found that religiously affiliated kids were more likely to be satisfied with their lives and with themselves as compared to non-religiously affiliated kids.[88]

One happiness researcher wondered if all the "thou shalt nots" of organized religion helps reduce confusion in the face of so many choices in contemporary life. Rabbi Harold Kushner, in *When Bad Things Happen to Good People,* writes that religion satisfies "the most fundamental human need of all. That is the need to know that somehow we matter, that our lives mean something, count as something more than just a momentary blip in the universe."[89] All of these ingredients may explain the greater frequency of self-reported happiness among religiously affiliated people.

Yet religion offers no fool-proof mechanism for attaining spirituality. The path of elevating heart and soul is open to all, believer or skeptic, religiously affiliated or secularist. Whatever brings out our best self, evokes our capacity for love and compassion and awe at the wonders and mysteries of the universe, whatever evokes our tenderness and acceptance of self and others—these are the stepping stones along the spiritual path we want to offer our children. Wise parents understand that they must lead the way.

13

Model Optimism

"There is nothing either good or bad, but thinking makes it so."
William Shakespeare

Almost five hundred years ago, William Shakespeare knew what contemporary research has demonstrated: our outlook makes all the difference in how we feel. And when it comes to attaining happiness, an optimistic outlook defeats the competition; it's one of the most dependable predictors of happiness.

What is an optimistic outlook? It's the expectation that problems are surmountable and that things will turn out okay—what some refer to as a "can do" attitude. Happy people have been found to swing into action when a problem arises: gathering resources, finding help, refusing to give up—the optimistic stance.[90] "The average unhappy person spends more than twice as much time thinking about unpleasant events in their lives, while happy people tend to seek and rely upon information that brightens their personal outlook."[91] Seligman's investigations have led him to believe that optimism lowers our vulnerability to depression and enhances productivity and physical health.[92] In *The Optimistic Child*, he reports on a study that found that the incidence of depression at the time of puberty was cut in half for 10-year-olds who were taught the skills of optimism.[93]

The value of optimism is most evident when life presents us with a challenge, when something knocks us off kilter and thrusts us into our discomfort zone. That's when we wonder, can I handle this? We can help our kids develop optimism in their ability to solve problems by giving them every opportunity, with our support and guidance, to take the lead in solving the problems that turn up in their own young lives. Prompting them with thought-provoking questions will grease the wheels of that capacity: "What do you think is the best way to handle this?" "How about if you list the pros and cons?" "If you were the parent, what would you do?" This gives them problem-solving practice, which in itself builds confidence. And to the extent that we can sometimes implement their suggestions and solutions, they will experience the *sense of control* in life that many researchers believe is a factor in good mental health.[94]

When there's no way to "fix" a disappointing situation or undo any damage done, whether accidental or not, outlook makes a difference. That's when the lesson of the day is *acceptance* rather than struggle, acceptance of an imperfect world where things don't always go our way. Acceptance, we must teach our children, doesn't signal defeat; it signals maturity. Similarly, asking for help doesn't signal failure; there's much we can't accomplish on our own. Lessons like these keep kids optimistic by teaching them to view tough moments through a more positive lens.

Research on older Americans has found that those with the greatest capacity to adapt to change—those with an optimistic outlook toward change—are the people most satisfied with their lives, while those who resist change are far less likely to feel happy.[95]

> Plant a Seed
> Teach your children that change can be good, that it can open up unexpected and wonderful pos-sibilities. It's an attitude that promotes an optimistic stance toward the change that is in-evitable in all our lives.

As parents, we must teach (and model) that when neg-ative events occur—setbacks, disappointments, mistakes and accidents—it's important not to assign personal blame *where it doesn't belong*. "I'm stupid." "It must be my fault." "If only I…" One study found that people who blame themselves regularly when things go wrong are far less likely to be satisfied in life than people who don't indulge in knee-jerk self-blame.[96] The key is being both realistic and gentle with ourselves.

From the time children crawl and smile and push a ball, parents can build a foundation of optimism through *recogni-tion*—noticing and commenting favorably on even the smallest successes. These are the moments when children feel satisfac-tion and pride: "Look what I can do!" (Recognition is discussed at length in Chapter 18.)

"You should remain alert to the fact that lots of success for your child will lead to optimism. You should go out of your way to help your child follow up one success with another, and another. The right coaching from you will support and maintain his optimism, and the right crucial experiences will set his optimism in concrete."[97]

How to discourage optimism? Approach everything as if it were a competition. If life is always a contest in which our children are expected to win, optimism easily gives way to pessimism, a sense of defeat even before they try. Children know they can't excel at everything; the pressure alone taints the joy of trying. But we're a society obsessed with winning: on the sports field, on television (reality programs, game shows), within the corporate culture. Many youngsters have been poisoned by the culture of competition and have adopted the attitude that "I won't try something new unless I know I'll be really good at it." Who wants to lose in a culture that esteems winning above all else?

How can parents counteract the disabling belief that only success counts? Two ways: first, by teaching that experience alone contains its own rewards—personal pleasures, stimulating challenges, the benefits and joys of learning—even without gold stars or trophies. And second, by embracing failure as the greatest of all learning experiences. "Failing is our best teacher," we must tell our children, and we must demonstrate patience and acceptance when things in their lives don't go their way, or when they make mistakes and fall flat on their faces. It's equally important that our kids see us bring patience and self-acceptance to our own moments of disappointment and failure.

> Plant a Seed
>
> Promote optimism in your child by giving voice to philosophies of resilience: "There's no problem we can't handle," or "That which doesn't kill me makes me stronger." Convey messages like these when they're young. Expose them to books like *The Little Engine That Could* and biographies about people who have persisted in the face of tough challenges.

Another way to promote optimism is by helping our kids develop *perspective*, the capacity to recognize the difference between what's big and what's small, what's major and what's minor. With perspective, children learn that most daily frustrations are "small stuff," nuisances and inconveniences no more egregious than an unexpected gust on a balmy day, rarely worth the emotional toll they can extract. We should refuse to catastrophize life's ordinary mishaps—"This is the end of *everything!*" or "I can't do *anything* right!"—and refuse to generalize from single mishaps and isolated misfortunes into global disasters—"*Nothing* ever works out for me!" We may not intend our words to be taken literally, but our children are listening; the expressions we use transmit to our kids lasting messages that shape their outlook.

> Plant a Seed
>
> Occasionally, at the dinner table, ask your children to name some small frustrations, disappointments, or setbacks that happened to them recently, as well as some big frustrations or setbacks. Talk about how we know the difference between what's big and what's small, and how our responses to those two categories ought to differ.

And finally, let's not forget the value of a sense of humor in promoting perspective and optimism. Find moments to laugh at yourself, at your foibles. Make a point of recounting, with plenty of light-hearted cheer, stories of your own misadventures; take delight when the kids chuckle with you. When they see you laugh in the face of minor adversities, they learn that few things are worth a sleepless night or a spoiled day.

14

Nurture Gratifying Pursuits

"Things won are done; joy's soul lies in the doing."
William Shakespeare

Happy people create gratifying and challenging activities for themselves, activities that are absorbing and often (but not always) pleasurable at the same time. They "lose themselves" in those activities, forgetting about the rest of life as time passes without notice. Being lost in an engaging activity has been labeled "flow," and it is an ingredient in the lives of many happy people.[98]

Neuroscience research confirms that gratifying, engaging activities stimulate the same areas of the brain as are stimulated by drugs. No wonder people engaged in joyful endeavors are so happy. (Substance use might be less appealing to youth if they found more sources of gratification and flow.)

What do we mean by a "gratifying activity?" Is it any different from so many activities that bring us pleasure and delight, like seeing a movie or shopping or roller-blading? In *Authentic Happiness*, Martin Seligman writes that our deepest sense of gratification and well-being comes not just from any pleasurable activity, but from those that exercise *signature strengths*.[99] He identifies 24 such strengths, including love of learning, valor and bravery, integrity and honesty, teamwork, and modesty. (See Appendix A for a complete list.) These strengths reflect the highest expression of human enterprise, the best qualities of character and engagement that men and women are capable of. While all 24 strengths can be developed and enhanced, people tend to shine more in some than in others. At the website www.authentichappiness.org, your children can take an online inventory to identify their top signature strengths. (There's an online inventory for you, too.) You can then use the information about your kids' top strengths to direct them toward activities that capitalize on those strengths. For instance, a daughter whose strengths include leadership, citizenship, and fairness might be encouraged to become involved in student government or youth politics, activities that are likely to be especially gratifying to her. A son whose strengths include humor and zest and a love of learning might be encouraged to join a children's comedy troupe or enroll in a class in humor writing. When the match is strong between our children's signature strengths and the activities they participate in—clubs and hobbies and extra-curricular programs—they are more likely to derive authentic happiness from those pursuits. Kids themselves can be shown how to use the knowledge of their signature strengths to find sources of true gratification at any age.

Not all pleasurable activities exercise the signature strengths, which doesn't mean we should discourage our children from, say, bike riding through the neighborhood on a lazy summer afternoon, or laying around after school listening to music. Simple pleasures and unstructured times of play make important contributions to happy lives; we must encourage and support our kids' pursuit of pleasure. But research has found that the benefits of simple pleasures are not as enduring as the benefits that derive from exercising our signature strengths. (We indicated earlier that exercising signature strengths may not always be pleasurable in the moment. Think of the mountain climber scaling a rough peak in harsh weather, or the swimmer straining every muscle to reach a personal best. Despite the absence of pleasure in every moment, the gratification from such endeavors may be intense and enduring nevertheless.)

Plant a Seed

Do what you can to encourage your children's natural talents and interests, especially those that exercise key signature strengths. Take the online Signature Strengths Inventory with your kids and together review and discuss the results. Help them find hobbies, classes, summer camps, and after school programs that support their interests and strengths.

Exposing children to a broad array of activities when they're young will help them discover one or more that will tickle their fancy and that can extend into adulthood as sources of pleasure and joy.

Some satisfying activities return a sense of pleasure quickly, without requiring carefully honed skills. Stamp collecting, reading, hiking, and jumping rope are just a few. Other activities—piano playing, ice skating, knitting, golf—depend on at least a minimal level of skill before the activity is truly pleasurable. Acquiring skill takes practice, and with practice we reach the point where pleasure sets in. That's what brings kids back for more—the pleasure. Here's where parents play a key role: insisting that children practice an activity long enough, during the tedious and frustrating early days, until the pleasure point is reached.

Once your children find sources of pleasure and gratification, teach them how to *savor* that pleasure, how to slow down and let the gratification ripple through and through. Savoring joy and pleasure has become all too rare. In these fast, multi-tasking times, it's easy to pass pleasure by, easy to race ahead rather than linger in the pleasure of where we are now, and where we've just been. How many of us fail to savor the flavors of a delicious meal because our eyes and ears are glued to the television while we're eating? How many of us fail to savor the pleasures of a country drive because a cell phone conversation has stolen our attention away? In his Positive Psychology seminar, Seligman teaches his students to savor pleasure by having them *take time* to relate wonderful experiences to others, and by keeping physical mementos of special events. The sight of mementos on the bookshelf or wall can trigger an emotional re-living of the original joy, a savoring. Parents can encourage children to telephone family and friends to describe recent pleasurable adventures, a savoring, and to keep a scrapbook of even the simplest delights. All the forms of savoring contribute to authentic happiness.

Plant a Seed

Two or three times a year, pull out photo albums or scrapbooks and gather the kids around to reminisce, reliving and savoring through memory the most enjoyable times.

Affluent families take heed. Research has found that kids from affluent homes are more likely to be bored and less likely to take pleasure from things than children growing up with fewer material indulgences.[100] Psychologists speculate that it has to do with the difference between *actively creating* versus *passively receiving* stimulation. Those who have received a lot—the passive recipients—may not have learned how to create their own sources of gratification and joy. They want to be entertained, preferably with bells and whistles, and aren't as resourceful using imagination to create pleasurable ways to pass the time. Teachers report that increasing numbers of students resist reading the long and challenging classics, finding the printed page insufficiently stimulating without colors and lights and motion. It's a concern that crosses all socio-economic classes nowadays as kids everywhere depend on quick, easy, and passive solutions to boredom: TV, computer, videogames and hand-held devices. The more our kids become passive-activity junkies, the harder it will be for them to create their own gratifying pursuits.

Nurture Gratifying Pursuits

We've looked at the eight *seeds*—good health, a life of meaning, closeness, acts of loving kindness, gratitude, spirituality, optimism, gratifying pursuits—that parents can plant to help their kids attain happy lives. But parents, like gardeners, must do more than plant; they must infuse key nutrients into the soil if they expect the seeds to flourish. Think about the soil in your children's lives—the atmosphere at home, the parent-child connection. Is it rich in the nutrients that kids require? From our review of the literature on raising healthy and happy children, we have distilled five ingredients—the essential nutrients—that experts agree contribute to the richest soil of all:[101]

- Connectedness
- Play
- Practice and mastery
- Recognition
- Self-control

In Part III, we will examine each nutrient in turn.

PART THREE

TILLING THE SOIL
OF AUTHENTIC HAPPINESS

15

Build Connectedness

"The only factor becoming scarce in a world of
abundance is human attention."
Kevin Kelly

This is it—the single most important nutrient on which happiness depends. Not to be confused with the closeness "seed" we discussed in Chapter 9, which has to do with friendship and connection with others, connectedness refers to the stable, reliable, and consistent *attachment* between a child and an adult that produces in the child a sense of feeling safe and loved. *Safe and loved.* Children who come through childhood with these feelings well-established enjoy what's been called "enduring core happiness."[102] It's a blessing indeed, enduring core happiness, providing an inner compass that assures, all through the lifespan, a sense of balance and stability even when we're tossing on life's rockiest waves.

> "While all people are likely to feel sad when they encounter everyday disappointments that occur in spite of their best effort, adults whose developmental needs [for safety and love] have been adequately satis-

fied…will not lose the inner happiness of feeling complete, lovable, and loved."[103]

How does a baby develop a sense of safety in this chaotic world? To answer that question, let's imagine ourselves inside the mind of the child, looking out from his or her perspective. When people *consistently* give me what I need—food, drink, warmth, stimulation—I'll begin to feel safe. Through the consistency, I'll develop a sense of trust *that what I need will be reliably provided*. If, on the other hand, my care is unpredictable—sometimes I go hungry and sometimes not, sometimes I'm handled roughly and sometimes not, sometimes I'm left to lay alone for long stretches without contact or touch, and sometimes not—I'll feel less safe, less trusting that the world will provide what I need.

An entire lifetime of relationship success—or disappointment—may hinge on this nutrient called connectedness. Brain scans of children who were severely neglected in infancy show inadequate development of the portion of the brain responsible for emotional attachments.[104] Some see this as evidence that babies who don't receive sufficient love and care may be permanently handicapped when it comes to connecting with people in love and friendship. The amount of joy in a toddler's life as a result of good caregiving, of rich and loving early connections, seems to establish critical brain pathways that make happiness possible all through life.[105]

A baby's basic needs are for food, drink, warmth, and stimulation—it's not that complicated, but the needs are relentless and non-stop. No matter how tired or distracted a parent might be, the baby's needs persist. How these needs are met sets the tone for the nature of early connectedness. Forget about the emphasis on just "quality time": when it comes to our youngest children, quantity is as important. A steady, reliable presence of key caregivers in the earliest years is necessary for a sense of safety to develop. Connectedness rarely forms when there's a revolving door of endlessly changing caregivers, each with a different way of holding and touching and soothing and feeding and diapering, no matter how skilled each might be.

Connectedness seems to instill a kind of optimism, the courage to go out into the world and face whatever comes our way. Connected kids feel a sense of being part of something larger than themselves, as though there's an *invisible* team behind them, lending support. But the invisible team only develops after years of being very *visible*: consistently and lovingly present in a child's life.

A few words about connectedness gone awry...

Across the planet, families look and act and think in a myriad of ways, yet adult-child connectedness occurs everywhere. Children of all cultures and communities have come to feel safe and loved whether they're swaddled in burlap across a mother's back, or ensconced in the rear of a Bentley. When it comes to connectedness, no particular advantage accrues to families with money or privilege. In fact, some wonder if children growing up within developed nations are reaching adolescence with less of a sense of being safe and loved than children from the developing world, where parents (especially mothers) have fewer options for how to spend their time, and so kids continue to receive huge amounts of consistent parental attention.

Yet, even when caregivers are physically present, connectedness can go awry, as it does regularly, everywhere. A parent's emotional problems represent the biggest threat as troubled parents are often inconsistent or emotionally absent, absorbed in problems of their own. Excessive alcohol or drug use can interfere with consistency: feedings may be late, an infant may be left too long to cry or returned to the crib before sufficient soothing has taken place. The ill-effects show up early: infants of depressed mothers have higher levels of stress hormones and lower levels of serotonin and dopamine, a profile linked to depression.[106] Children as young as three or four may have to fend for themselves when a parent's impairment makes it hard to get out of bed and tend to the youngsters. In all these ways, a child's sense of being safe in the world—"I have confidence my needs will be met"—may not fully develop.

And then there are chaotic adult relationships: parents who yell or hit or curse or smash objects against the wall. What child can feel safe when emotions spill over recklessly? (We're talking about *chronic* patterns of frightening behavior, not the rare instance in which mature, stable parents lose their footing.) Connectedness is always compromised when a child lives in a state of fear, wondering when trouble will erupt.

What of family break-up? How does it impact a child's future happiness? Research presents a solid case for the deleterious effects of divorce. Some say the break in family composition, a kind of earthquake in the child's foundation, disrupts any sense of security the child may have developed; for some kids, the ground never again feels quite as stable. In one of many studies on the topic, kids of divorce were nearly twice as likely to become depressed during adulthood as kids whose parents remained together, regardless of the child's age at the time of the separation.[107] Knowing this, some couples try to stay together for the kids' sake. But if parental conflict is too severe, it may be in the children's interest for the parents to part ways.[108] Regardless of the path families take—staying together or moving apart—doing everything possible to *preserve connections* and promote children's sense of feeling safe and loved ought to be high priorities for parents.

Parent-child connectedness can be enhanced through unconditional love. Unconditional love is a blend of attitude and spirit that conveys a deep affection for and commitment to our children despite their being naughty at age four, disobedient at age ten, and surly at age fifteen. We may not like what they've said or done, we may be angry and frustrated and disappointed with them, but we still love them—*and they know it*. They feel it. Even as we admonish them for their misdeeds and poor choices, even as we impose consequences when they've done wrong, they know that our caring and commitment never waver. That's unconditional love.

If you're unsure whether you're conveying unconditional love, you might ask your children (although they may only give you the answer they think you want to hear). Ask: Does it ever feel to you that I take my love away? Does it ever feel to you that I'm so angry or upset that I don't care about you anymore, even for a little while?

If our own parents didn't offer us unconditional love, it may not be easy to offer it to our kids. It's an attitude that seems to pass from one generation to the next. But it can be developed. Here's how:

First, always criticize the behavior, never the person: "I don't like when you tease your brother," "That's not the right thing to do," "Lying is wrong." Focus your anger on what they've done, not on who they are.

Second, swear-off all personal put-downs: "You're stupid!" "You're bad!" "Shame on you!" "You jerk!" "You'll never amount to anything." Words like these are absolutely unloving, uncaring, and disrespectful. Most of us wouldn't speak to a sales clerk that way; why should our children receive less consideration? (If you find yourself unable to break the habit of put-downs and disparaging remarks, seek professional help. These habits are often tough to change on our own.)

Third, even the most skilled parents can slip, can say or do the wrong thing in a moment of pique or when a child is exceptionally provocative. When you've slipped—we all do!—apologize. Say you're sorry. Let your kids know you recognize that you've done wrong, that *their feelings matter to you* and you regret having hurt them. Your sincere apology can usually heal the wound.

Many parents are surprised when we talk about the importance of connectedness in the lives of older children, during the pre-teen and adolescent years. Older kids so often seem to resist connectedness, resist family time and prefer to hole up in their rooms. While youngsters' needs change as they move toward and through adolescence, connectedness with parents remains important nonetheless. Data from the National Longitudinal Study of over 9,000 students in grades seven through twelve found that teens who felt connected both at home and at school (school connectedness includes feeling close to and getting along well with teachers and students) were less likely to experience emotional problems, depression, drug or alcohol use, unwanted pregnancy, or to drop out of high school.[109] Even academic success seems tied to connectedness: a study of 1,000 students at an elite east coast prep school found that the best grades were earned by the most connected students, not the most academically-driven students.[110]

Teenagers need (and want) to know that their parents are nearby, thinking about them. They need parents to ask about their lives and their whereabouts, even to insist on family time together. It's disturbing that over the past twenty years, family time—parents and kids together—has been occurring less and less. Between 1981 and 1997, the amount of time family members spend just talking to each other decreased by half.[111] This does not bode well for our children's sense of connectedness. But what's most surprising is that *kids themselves are unhappy about it.* One study found that 33% of children between the ages of 9 and 17 wished their parents spent less time working and more time with them.[112] Is it any wonder that President Bush proclaimed a national Family Day in September 2005, calling on people to spend time with family members and reaffirming the important relationship between parents and children? Imagine the puzzled looks all around had such a proclamation been issued in our grandparents' era.

> Till the Soil
>
> Promote connectedness by listening to your kids, paying serious attention to what's on their minds. If you need to, ask questions to draw them out—when you're driving them to a friend's, while you're fixing dinner and they meander through the kitchen. Listen without advising, without criticizing, without helping. (There's time for that later.) Remember how effective empathy can be in helping them feel safe and understood, and in encouraging them to open up with you. And remember to share of yourself with them; it's not a one-way street. If *your* inner life—hopes and dreams, fears and disappointments—is completely closed off from them, don't be surprised if they close theirs off from you.

Parents don't often acknowledge how tired they are after a long day at work, and after taking care of the family's basic needs: groceries, laundry, household chores. There seems so little time and energy for the kids, beyond "Have you done your homework?" or "Ten minutes till bedtime." Parents easily rationalize the time crunch by telling themselves that connectedness doesn't matter as much once kids reach a certain age. Perhaps you're one of the parents who underestimates the impact of your absences and overestimates the degree of closeness your children feel with you.[113] Don't fool yourself.

Till the Soil

Have dinner with your children as often as you can. Few other activities offer as good an opportunity to show interest in their lives. Dinnertime together is a powerful way for kids to feel nurtured and cared for by you, no matter how old they are; it doesn't matter if the meal is homemade or brought in. Research shows that *not* eating dinner as a family raises your children's risk two- or three-fold for early sex, drug use, and emotional problems.[114]

And let's not fool ourselves into believing that quality time trumps quantity time once kids reach adolescence. Connectedness demands that we be present—even for our teens, even though they may be behind a closed door, instant messaging their friends and seemingly oblivious to us. Still, they know we're there; their leash is shorter; their shaky adolescent impulses can't as easily range far afield. They're feeling safer.

"Being there" doesn't just mean showing up to watch the Saturday afternoon soccer game. That's a performance, not an opportunity for connection. Meaningful moments of connection happen unexpectedly, when parents and kids are just hanging out and a son or daughter opens up and shares something personal, something important. Something that might only be expressed *when the time is right.*

If you value connectedness, say so: tell your children how important it is to you. Create ritualized ways of being together, such as family movie night, Sunday breakfast, regular family outings. Bring everyone together and make a fuss over birthdays and graduations and even "ordinary" milestones like learning to ride a bike, baking a first cake, receiving a fine report card. Read together with the children for as many years as they'll let you. One study found parent-child reading to correlate with higher SAT scores.

It's estimated that 70% of 9–17-year-olds have a television in their bedroom;[115] 30% of the 0-3-year-olds and 40% of the 4-6-year-olds also have televisions in their bedroom.[116] Nielsen Media Research found that American children spend about 24 hours each week watching TV. Is it a good thing? Not if it encourages kids to isolate themselves from the rest of the family. Don't be afraid to remove the bedroom television, to acknowledge that it may have been a mistake to allow it in the first place if it functions to keep family members apart. Computers can do the same thing, of course. Online chats with friends have replaced the telephone, and surfing the net has come to occupy more and more time in our children's lives (and in our own). Don't be afraid to insist on limits on the use of technology when it starts interfering with a reasonable amount of family time. (Years ago, pleasurable family time included everyone around the television, not the solitary viewing—each person in a different room—seen in so many homes today.)

Till the Soil

It's not unusual anymore for parents to be as plugged in as their kids to TV screens and computer monitors. The problem isn't so much what you are doing as what you're *not* doing: conversations, meals, outings, any activity where you're engaged side-by-side. Consider reading some of the books your middle- and high-schoolers are assigned in their English or literature classes. Discuss the books with them at dinner or when you're driving in the car, not as a quiz on what they know, but as a means of feeling close by sharing their experience.

But most of all—yes, we're repeating ourselves here—strive for family meals. One study found that families who eat together five or more times a week have children with higher grade-point averages, less depression, and less alcohol and substance use than children in families who eat together two or fewer times a week.[117] Psychologist Dan Kindlon speculates that of all family rituals, this one carries a deep resonance for children, recreating at the dinner table the sense of safety and soothing that they felt at the beginning of their lives, when they were held in our arms during their first feedings.

16

Cherish Play

*"It is the child in man that is the source of his uniqueness
and creativeness, and the playground is the optimal milieu
for the unfolding of his capacities and talents."*

Eric Hoffer

N
o other *activity* of early childhood is more important
in laying a foundation for later happiness than *play*.
What exactly do we mean by play? It's anything
a child does that allows for spontaneity and creativity. Any activity that, as it flows along, transforms itself according to a
child's imagination and impulse. (One way to know play is by
its opposite: doing exactly as we are told.[118]) When a two-year-
old sits in front of a kitchen cabinet pulling plastic Tupperware
containers off the shelf, watching them tumble into a heap, tossing them left and right, pushing them with the palm of his hand
and watching them roll across the floor—that's play. It's spontaneous; it's imaginative; the child invents the "rules" (until
some grown-up comes along with a different notion of what's
permissible). When several five-year-olds decide to play
"house," assigning roles and tasks according to whim and
imagination ("Let's invite the bears to tea!"), inventing the rules

as they go along ("I'll be the Mommy and you be the sister")—
that's play. When nine-year-olds declare themselves a "club"
on a lazy summer afternoon, then go exploring together for
bugs and rocks and imaginary villains in the empty lot across
the street—that's play. Play comes naturally to kids when left
to their own devices, using whatever happens to be around to
fashion a "game" according to their ever-inventive imaginations.

What makes play a crucial stepping stone toward later
happiness? In unstructured play, children discover the power
to amuse themselves. They learn to use imagination to turn
possibilities into realities—with twigs or blocks or dolls or
trucks. The child at play discovers that so much begins with a
thought, *his* or *her* thought, and that with some effort and re-
sourcefulness, he can make things happen; she can create her
own joy. What power! What fun! Absorbed in play as the minutes click by, children experience the earliest form of flow.

Till the Soil

Don't be afraid of boredom.
Don't think you need to remedy
your kids' bored moments with
a buffet of activity choices. "I'm
bored" often serves as the prelude to the exercise of imagination and creativity, an
opportunity for play. "I'm
bored" offers our kids a chance
to practice reflection, which is
how they learn about them-

> selves, how they visualize the future, how they rehearse, in their minds, some of the challenges that lay ahead.

Life at play rarely proceeds without setbacks and annoyances, frustrations and disappointments. That's how play is real life in microcosm, which lends it particular power as a training ground for the world outside. Children at play can learn to tolerate frustration and solve problems: when the block tower falls, she can build it up again. When it falls a second time, she'll feel frustrated and angry. She might turn away, but if she stacks the blocks more slowly and they remain standing, she'll discover that she has the power within herself to succeed. When a child plays with others, he begins to learn about cooperation, about what's involved in getting along. He learns that there are advantages and disadvantages of including others in play.

Respect the psychological seriousness of play to the child, even when it looks frivolous and silly from the outside. Don't demand that play come to a halt on a moment's notice just because *you're* ready to sit down to dinner. Give a five or ten-minute warning; let your children bring their play to meaningful closure or pause.

The mid-twentieth century may have been the golden era of play, before workaholism supplanted leisure, before boredom became a sin, and before huge amounts of television-watching and electronic game-playing shaped a generation or two of *passive* participants. Since the mid-twentieth century, an achievement-obsessed society has produced achievement-obsessed parents, pushing children to develop skills at earlier and earlier ages, whether it's identifying the ABCs at three or performing a back flip at seven. All this emphasis on "personal development" takes time away from real play. High-tech "educational" toys and games masquerade as play with all their bells and whistles, but real play—spontaneous and creative—is something quite different.

Observers of trends in children's behavior often note the absence of youngsters up and down the residential streets after school and on weekends, even in the safest neighborhoods.[119] The once familiar image of kids riding bicycles together, playing hopscotch or four square or simply hanging out, has been replaced in most areas by empty sidewalks and quiet side streets. It's not just parents' heightened safety concerns that explain this change over 30 or 40 years. Kids today tend to be indoors—in front of TV or a video screen, or in organized classes and activities—none of which constitute real play.

Is play destined for extinction, squeezed out by the cultural obsession with productivity and achievement? One study found that children's free time—the time available to play—has declined 16% between 1981 and 1997.[120] Athletics has absorbed some of this time, but organized sports, focused so much on winning, fail to meet the definition of true play. As parents (and as a society), we must be mindful and protective of children's need for play, particularly with neuroscience research suggesting that "our brain comes hardwired with an urge to play."[121]

A nutrient-rich soil includes plenty of time for play.

Till the Soil

Limit the amount of time your kids sit in front of a computer monitor or TV screen becoming high-stimulation junkies, getting hooked on constantly changing scenes, fast action, bright colors and quirky sounds. True play requires time and space and the absence of distracting background noise, so our kids can hear themselves think, can hear the wheels of their own imagination turning.

17

Require Practice and Mastery

"Practice, the master of all things."
Augustus Octavius

How many practice swings does it take until Emma learns to connect the bat with the ball? How many wrong notes until Jesse's fingers master the C major scale? Doing something over and over again—how frustrating and discouraging it can be. No wonder children balk. But only through *practice* can they reach a certain level of skill and, once at that level, begin to taste the pleasures of *mastery*.

Practice and mastery—these are the nutrients in the childhood soil that support, as kids get older, gratifying work and engaging hobbies. As we saw in Chapter 14, so many happy adults know how to find sources of joy and gratification. They're able to do so because as youngsters, practice and mastery taught them how to stick with something long enough to derive pleasure from it, whether it be golf, bridge, drawing, civic involvement or community theater.

Practice teaches kids other important lessons, as well. Because we're rarely effective on our first or third or fifth attempt, practice produces frustration, a kind of adversity. That's a good thing. Without frustration, we could never develop frustration tolerance. Without frustration, we couldn't learn the value of persistence, pushing forward despite the temptation to throw in the towel. Practice teaches that only through effort do we reach the payoff.

Parents tell us how quickly many kids lose interest once frustration sets in. A daughter throws down the tennis racket and declares, "I hate this game." A son shoves back from assembling the puzzle and complains, "It's too hard." For the moment, they're defeated, and if we only want them to be happy, we're tempted to let them turn their backs on what was hard. But there's an unfortunate lesson learned when kids engage in serial starting-and-stopping, like a hummingbird flitting from one flower to the next. Too many learn to give up when the ride gets rough; they turn to something new rather than persist to the point of accomplishment and satisfaction.

> Till the Soil
> Join in as a kind of empathic cheerleader on those occasions when your son or daughter, engaged in some activity, reaches the point of frustration and wants to throw in the towel. Acknowledge their frustration while you commend their perseverence thus far. "Maybe I can help you figure out that hard part," you can offer when assembling the short-wave radio has

> severely tried your son's pa-
> tience. "Why don't you keep at it
> for a little while longer," you can
> suggest, "and then let's go out
> for an ice-cream cone to celebrate
> your hard work."

Remember: mastery doesn't mean perfection. It simply refers to attaining a basic level of competence in whatever we do. Virtually every child can learn to ride a bike, throw a ball, bake cookies or paint a fence. In every instance, there's mastery.

> "Do not set standards that are too high or too low. If you expect nothing—if your standards are too low—then your child will get the message that you do not think he can do much, and he may likely agree. On the other hand, if you set standards that are way beyond what your child is capable of, then he may spend his entire life trying to live up to what you expect, never getting there, and will always feel dissatisfied with his efforts. This is one of the most common reasons for un-happiness among high achievers."[122]

Pushing children to persevere until they experience even limited mastery pays huge rewards. (Sometimes kids re-quire our help, sometimes only our encouragement to stay the course.) Mastery fuels the confidence that translates into a kind of optimism: "I know I can achieve when I put my mind to it, when I hang in long enough." Sticking with something challenging that they'd rather avoid, a kind of stress, is one way kids develop resilience in the face of frustration. One research team found that laboratory animals who effectively bounced back from stress during adulthood—those who showed re-silience—were the animals exposed to stress when they were young. "We can learn to be resilient [when we're young] by being exposed to a threat or stress at a level that allows us to manage it," says neuroscientist Richard Davidson.[123] It's the practice that makes all the difference.

When is it best *not* to push a child to stick with an ac-tivity, just for the sake of practice? There are no hard and fast rules that apply across the board, but one helpful guideline seems to be this: push your children to stick with activities and pursuits that provide a strong match with either their innate talents or their signature strengths (see Chapter 14). Those are the pursuits that inevitably return the greatest degree of pleas-ure and gratification, if not today then tomorrow; those are the pursuits that are worth your children's sticking with despite the tedium of practice. For example, if your daughter wants to quit the after-school gymnastics program and you recognize, after an honest appraisal, that she has only minimal athletic tal-ent, your energy may be better spent helping her identify an activity that better matches her talents and signature strengths than in pushing her to practice the parallel bars. Do the same with a son who complains constantly about having to practice the clarinet and you recognize, after an honest appraisal, that he has only minimal musical talent. When children have not found activities that build on their innate talents or draw suffi-ciently from their signature strengths, you may want to help them find a better match rather than persist with their current activity—and once you've found the match, push them to practice.

Practice leads to mastery and mastery to confidence, creating a reservoir of "can-do" optimism and hope from which children will draw later in life when they attempt something challenging and new. It is a reservoir that contributes to a great many contented and thriving lives.

18

Offer Recognition

"Praise the young and they will flourish."
Irish proverb

We till the soil with our recognition: our smiles of approval, our shouts of joy, our words of commendation. Recognition lets our kids know they've done well, that their efforts delight us. It "can make the difference between joyless achievement and joyful mastery."[124]

Repeated many times, the sound of our recognition becomes internalized by our kids: they learn to offer themselves the same approval that they hear from us, a kind of internal chorus. (Similarly, if it's scorn and disapproval they receive from us, then scorn and disapproval is the song their chorus sings.)

What should recognition sound like? Psychologists have found that optimal praise commends effort and accomplishment, not inborn traits like intelligence or athleticism. It's better to say, "What a great job you did!" or "You really gave that a good try!" or "I like the way you passed the ball to your teammates" rather than "You're so smart!" or "You're so coordinated!" It seems that when we only praise traits of birth—

you're beautiful, you're smart, you're talented—without commending effort and application, many kids develop a sense that what matters most are the gifts they're born with, not what they do with those gifts—not how they apply themselves.

In studies of achievement motivation, kids praised for being "smart" were found to care more about "looking good" (maintaining the "smart" identity) than about what they actually learned. After an experience of failure, those same kids gave up more quickly on subsequent tasks, reported less enjoyment of the tasks, and saw themselves as less capable than a group of kids who had initially been praised for their effort, rather than their "smarts."[125]

Till the Soil

Be generous with your recognition but don't flood your child with praise. Youngsters can become too dependent on the approval of others and lose the capacity for quiet, private *self*-approval. Occasionally, when your son or daughter approaches you and says, "How did I do?" ask first how *they* think they did, a self-evaluation. After they've given an adequate response, add your two cents' worth of recognition.

Avoid, too, another kind of recognition that has been widely promoted in the past few decades: "You're special!" "You're great!" and "You're the best!" Proponents of this kind of recognition argued that our children would come to feel good about themselves simply by hearing others tell them how wonderful they are. We call this "empty" recognition, disconnected from anything the kids may say or do. Empty recognition celebrates children for no other reason than that they are alive. Of course, parents *should* celebrate their children just for being alive, but that is best conveyed through statements like, "I love you," and "You're special to me." For the most part, recognition should be parceled out based on *effort* ("I'm proud of you for sticking with that task!"), *achievement* ("Your performance was just beautiful!"), and especially evidence of *good character* ("I'm so impressed with how considerate you are of others!" or "Your honesty makes me the happiest parent in the world!"). One author sees non-specific, universal praise—messages like "You're great!"—as a mistaken way some parents attempt to show unconditional love:

> "Offering praise has become a sort of panacea for the anxieties of modern parenting...Out of our children's lives from breakfast to dinner, we turn it up a notch when we get home. In those few hours together, we want them to hear the things we can't say during the day—*We are in your corner, we are here for you, we believe in you.*"[126]

Recognition can start early: when kids take their first steps, utter their first words, play appropriately with a toy. Our recognition insinuates us into their lives as an important source of their satisfaction, and once we become a source of satisfaction, we carry weight and influence. They develop the habit of thinking about us, wondering what our reaction will be to the things they do. This event in their development, the internalizing of us, is significant in a number of ways.

First, our presence in our kids' thoughts reinforces their sense of connectedness. We've become important; thinking about us promotes their sense of being part of a team, parent and child together.

Second, our recognition promotes hopefulness in them about their capacity to accomplish and achieve. This contributes to self-confidence and optimism.

Third, many psychologists believe that the root of moral behavior rests in the child's interest and delight in the parent's approving reactions. The parent's recognition feels so good that the child desires it and therefore seeks it out. The parent's opinion becomes a moral compass, pointing the child in preferred directions. "I don't want to violate the norms and ethics of the people I care about."

Fourth, our recognition conveys to children a sense that what they do has meaning above and beyond the activity itself. When we smile and express delight at the Lego structure Darryl has created, he learns that his efforts are more than fun— they are a way of pleasing the people around him, the people who matter. The message is that what he's doing has worth, has purpose. This becomes the forerunner of the "seed" we discussed in Chapter 8: creating a life of meaning.

19

Teach Self-Control

"Formula of my happiness: a Yes, a No, a straight line, a goal."
Friedrich Nietzsche

More than ever, the culture presents a constant stream of temptations, material and experiential: larger TVs, exotic vacations, fancier cars. For youngsters, temptations include the latest videogames, the newest model cell phone, the cool athletic shoes. Every day, advertising serves up another helping of the state-of-the-art, must-have stuff. But happiness research, as we have seen, tells us that it's not the people collecting the stuff who are the happiest, not the people whose long hours at the workplace go toward funding endless consumption. Rather, the happiest people practice gratitude for what they have, *resisting* the siren call of rampant consumerism. They understand that they can never have enough of the things they don't really need.[127]

How do they resist all the temptation, these happy people?

In part, through *self-control*: the capacity to regulate one's needs and wants and emotions. Self-control is that aspect of maturity that enables us to tolerate frustration ("This is difficult, but I won't throw in the towel"), to delay gratification ("I don't need to have it immediately"), to control our emotions ("I won't throw a tantrum, won't kick and scream"), and, as we've said, to resist temptation ("I can choose to turn away, even though it calls to me").

> "My wife and I talk about our big spending decisions at the dinner table," says a father of four. "We debate the merits of putting our money into a vacation versus replacing something in the house that needs repair. The children learn that we can't do it all, that we have to make some sacrifices. I used to think that these conversations ought to take place privately, just my wife and me. But I've learned about the value to the kids in hearing how we weigh and measure our own spending decisions, so they can see that we can't have it all."

For self-control to develop, parents have to set limits, impose clear guidelines, apply consequences, and in so many ways say "no." Of course, "no" tends to make kids *un*happy, and if you only want your kids to be happy, you're going to have a hard time teaching self-control. It requires a serious approach to discipline, which is a topic, in its particulars, outside the scope of this book. Many fine books are available that address this important topic. Suffice it to say that self-control is an important precursor to authentic happiness. Our children must be taught *not* to throw a tantrum when their needs aren't met. (If they do, there are consequences, like a time-out or a loss of privileges.) They must learn to accept "no" without creating big and pointless dramas. (Oscar-worthy performances earn them consequences.) All kids must learn to express difficult feelings—upset, hurt, anger, sadness—through appropriate words, not through physical or verbal aggression. ("I'm glad that you told me you're angry," says the wise parent. "But I'm still not extending your bedtime.") Over time, with parent's ongoing limit-setting, children eventually set these limits for themselves, in their own minds—this is self-control—without needing the parent's reminder.

> **Till the Soil**
> Set an example of self-control for your children. Deny yourself in the face of temptation, and let your children see it. "That jacket in the window is so nice, but I don't really need it." Or, "I'd really like a new car stereo, but it's not in the budget." Do the same with food—"That sundae looks delicious, but I've had enough to eat"—and with frustration in general—"It's no pleasure waiting in this long line, but we'll make the best of it."

Teaching children self-control has indeed become harder in recent decades with the popularity of the happiness creed. In psychologist Kindlon's Parenting Practices at the Millennium Study, 50% of parents reported being less strict than their own parents were; presumably, they are saying "no" to their own kids much less often than their parents said to them.[128] (It's not surprising that a high percentage of the youth questioned in that study identified themselves as "spoiled." Isn't being spoiled in some ways the result of too much "yes" and too little "no"?) Certainly it can be hard on parents when sons and daughters press for the same material goods or opportunities that their friends enjoy. Keeping up with the Jones's children is an unwelcome pressure felt by kids and parents alike, making it all that tougher for parents to say "no."

> "We've become a culture of 'yes-parents' who don't want to see our children unhappy for a single minute. Guilty about our allocation of work time versus family time, so many of us downplay the importance of discipline, trying to maximize harmony at home; saying 'no' seems only to spoil that. And sometimes, thinking about the kids' misdeeds, and executing appropriate consequences, feels too draining after a long day. Who has the energy?"[129]

And yet, can there be any more important use of our energy than in tilling the soil of our sons and daughters' lives, an investment today that returns value well into the future—for us, for them, and for the generations that we can only dream about.

20

Consider Character

"Character is higher than intellect."
Ralph Waldo Emerson

Y
ou may, by now, have identified the paradox at the heart of our message: to help your children achieve happiness, let it go. Release it from your thoughts. Know that happiness is a side-effect, a by-product of living our lives in certain ways; it can't be forced or planned. If happiness is your fondest wish for your kids, *embrace the wish and let it go*—that's the paradox. Let the planting and tilling be your focus, not the words of an empty creed.

For three decades, parents have been telling us that they just want their kids to be happy. And for three decades, we have witnessed moms and dads putting that belief into practice, with all the negative consequences we have described in this book. But at times, some of those parents have conveyed something else, something that betrayed the primacy of the happiness wish. We heard it in the distress of a mother when she learned that her "queen bee" middle school daughter had been terrorizing several socially awkward girls in the class. We heard it in the upset of a father when he learned that his fifth grade son had been vandalizing the walls of the school bathrooms. And we heard it in the devastation of one couple when they learned that their teenager had hurled angry obscenities at his athletic coach during a post-game reprimand. The strong reactions of these parents to their children's misdeeds told us that there *is*, for many families, something equal to—maybe even more important than—grades or sports or popularity, more important even than a child's happiness. Perhaps it's important to you, too.

Imagine the following:

You've passed on from this world to a place called heaven. From there, you can look down on the lives of your loved ones. Make believe you have three children: A, B, and C. From heaven, here's what you observe:

Child A is a corporate CEO who received a doctorate from a prestigious graduate school and went on to form a successful biotech company. She is both wealthy and powerful in her industry and beyond. But from your heavenly perch, you hear that she is regarded by colleagues and friends as a haughty and difficult person. Co-workers describe her as arrogant and lacking compassion; some question her honesty.

Child B owns a successful chain of shops adjacent to beaches throughout Hawaii, renting scuba, snorkeling, and surfing gear to tourists. From your heavenly perch, you see that he is undeniably happy. His stress-free business allows him time to leave his shops in the care of store managers most afternoons to go off surfing. He lives alone, has little desire for close friendship, and endorses the motto, "Live and let live." Employees say he's "hard to get to know," that he shows little interest in them or in anything beyond his own immediate concerns.

Child C teaches fourth grade at a public elementary school. From your heavenly perch, you overhear her colleagues talk about what a pleasure she is to work with, considerate and respectful. Parents commend her loving and caring style with the children. Friends regard her as a person of integrity and cherish her friendship.

Which child would fill you, at the end of your days, with the greatest sense of pride?

For the authors of this book, and for many parents we have spoken with, the answer is C—the child with the finest character. Of course, there's no denying the satisfaction when a son or daughter achieves wealth or fame, fulfillment or happiness. But most parents tell us that the finest accomplishments lose their luster when a child lacks the qualities of a good and decent person. Indeed, for many moms and dads, *character matters*. Some don't realize how much it matters until its absence stares them in the face: the call from a neighbor or the principal, or, worse yet, the police, when a child does wrong. That may be the first time those parents talk about—even think about—the role of character in their children's lives. That may be when parents who have allowed character to slide down the hierarchy of what's important rethink their priorities, reconsider the value messages they are transmitting to their kids. It often takes a wake-up call before moms and dads preach the character virtues alongside good grades or a rich social life.

The near-silence in so many homes when it comes to character reflects, perhaps more than anything, the ethos of our consumer culture, where surface trumps depth and fun trumps meaning. Too many of us look at our kids and see what's on the outside, not what's on the inside. That shouldn't surprise us; for decades, parents preoccupied with character have been regarded as embarrassingly old-fashioned, out of step with the times. It wasn't always so. In the early and middle decades of the last century, parents weren't afraid to fuss about character. Government, education, and business leaders—not just ministers, priests and rabbis—weren't reluctant to lend their voice to particular core values. History and civics textbooks devoted long sections to the meaning of good citizenship; friends and neighbors felt free to reprimand each other's children and deliver a message about what's right. No longer. Character rarely finds its way into popular discourse, drowned out by the voices of allegiance to our kids' happiness. Harry R. Lewis, former dean of Harvard College, writes in *Excellence Without a Soul: How a Great University Forgot Education*, that universities are permeated by "today's consumer culture, in which the college's job is to make its students happy rather than to educate them...nothing in Harvard's curriculum was held to be more important for Harvard students to learn than anything else...a formula they hoped would please their students."[130] It's not that different at home: parents softening the demand for moral and ethical behavior while striving to keep kids happy.

And so our children are growing up in homes that emphasize grades and sports and shopping and *happiness*, not respect, compassion, honesty, empathy, courage, maturity, altruism, responsibility, and self-control. Most children never hear their parents utter the words spoken by Earl Woods when asked to comment on the success of his son, Tiger, who had just won the prestigious Masters Tournament. "My greatest satisfaction," said this proud father, "is that he's a good person."[131] Imagine if *all* kids heard their parents speak this way, if all kids understood that it is their character that matters most to mom and dad. Imagine a society in which children answered our original survey question—"What do your parents most want you to be?"—not with happy or smart or successful, but with good. *Good*—the choice that received only eight percent of the votes in our middle school survey!

Yes, you say, but does this talk of character have a place in a book about how to guide our kids toward happy lives?

We believe it does, and we're not the first to say so. Over two thousand years ago, Aristotle espoused a connection between the happy life and a life of virtue. Some scholars and philosophers have echoed that viewpoint ever since. Most recently, Seligman's thesis that authentic happiness requires the exercise of signature strengths—these strengths are undeniably dimensions of character—resurrects within psychology a conversation about character that fell out of favor during the last hundred years. Apparently, the wisdom of centuries wasn't all wrong. The happiness studies reviewed in earlier chapters imply a great deal about character, even though scientists haven't interpreted their findings through that lens.

Consider, for instance, the role of closeness (the third seed) in shaping happy lives. Who is likely to realize and sustain the most rewarding relationships—the person who is honest and compassionate and empathic with friends and family, or the person lacking those *traits of character*? Consider acts of loving kindness (the fourth seed). Who is likely to engage in such acts—the person who is generous and altruistic and empathic toward others, or the person lacking those *traits of char-*

147

acter? Consider gratitude, spirituality, and a life of meaning. A close and careful look at all of the eight seeds reveals the presence of character in each and every one of them.

And we must not forget that *our* children are the future parents of the next generation; our children will someday be tilling the soil for their own offspring. Qualities of character—patience, empathy, maturity, self-control, compassion—will make a certain difference when our sons and daughters become the gardeners in their own children's lives. What we do to shape their characters today will reverberate through generations.

Philosophers through the ages have agreed that everyone seeks happiness—youth and adults alike. But not everyone seeks to improve his or her character. Young people in particular rarely aim their thoughts that way. It's an education they can only receive at the hands of others, before they reach maturity and before the die has been cast. And so it falls to wise and loving parents to undertake the task: to plant the seeds and till the soil and *shape fine character* in their sons and daughters. Authentic happiness, for both generations, will be the glorious reward.

What parents should think & say:

- I want them to have good health.
- I want them to find meaning.
- I want them to enjoy closeness.
- I want them to practice acts of loving kindness.
- I want them to know gratitude.
- I want them to be spiritual.
- I want them to be optimistic.
- I want them to find gratifying pursuits.
- I want them to have fine character.

Appendix A

The Signature Strengths

We offer here a list of the twenty-four strengths, as found in Martin Seligman's book, *Authentic Happiness* (New York: Free Press, 2002). Expanded definitions of these strengths can be found in Dr. Seligman's book and in *Character Strengths and Virtues: A Handbook and Classification*, by Christopher Peterson and Martin Seligman (New York: Oxford University Press, 2004).

Wisdom and Knowledge
1. Curiosity/Interest in the World
2. Love of Learning
3. Judgment/Critical Thinking/Open Mindedness
4. Ingenuity/Originality/Practical Intelligence/Street Smarts
5. Social Intelligence/Personal Intelligence/Emotional Intelligence
6. Perspective

Courage
7. Valor and Bravery
8. Perseverance/Industry/Diligence
9. Integrity/Genuineness/Honesty

Humanity and Love
10. Kindness and Generosity
11. Loving and Allowing Oneself To Be Loved

Justice

12. Citizenship/Duty/Teamwork/Loyalty
13. Fairness and Equity
14. Leadership

Temperance

15. Self-Control
16. Prudence/Discretion/Caution
17. Humility and Modesty

Transcendence

18. Appreciation of Beauty and Excellence
19. Gratitude
20. Hope/Optimism/Future-Mindedness
21. Spirituality/Sense of Purpose/Faith/Religiousness
22. Forgiveness and Mercy
23. Playfulness and Humor
24. Zest/Passion/Enthusiasm

Appendix B

Planting & Tilling At-A-Glance

For easy reference, we have consolidated the 26 *Plant a Seed* and *Till the Soil* suggestions, presented here in the order in which they appear in the text.

Teach the Habits of Good Health

1. Teach your children, by words and example, to value good health and the habits that promote it: moderation and balance in work and play, healthful eating, regular exercise, adequate sleep, and the avoidance of cigarettes and excessive alcohol.

2. Let your children hear you talk about challenging feelings and difficult moods: "I've been feeling sad lately, ever since Grandma died," or "All day long I've been upset about the damage I did to the car yesterday," or "I've been pretty grumpy lately, maybe because I haven't been sleeping well at night." And let them hear you describe the constructive ways you are handling those feelings. "I've been talking to people at work about Grandma's death, and it seems to help me feel better," or "I know my upset will pass, as it always does," or "I'll phone my doctor and see if I can get some help with that sleep problem."

Appendix B

Promote a Life of Meaning

3. Talk with your children about the importance of living life with a sense of purpose. Share with them the sources of meaning in your own life, and invite friends and family, when the kids are around, to talk about their own sources of meaning. Ask your kids who they admire in the world, and why. Tell them whom you have admired, and talk about the people who have been cultural heroes in the past.

4. Help your children feel part of something larger than themselves, a chain of humanity. And help them understand that all of us stand on the shoulders of those who came before us, who made a difference through their own meaningful lives. Keep meaningful mementos and photographs of ancestors around the house; create a family tree. Visit the gravesites of family members and talk about the values dear to them, what they stood for. Educate your kids about the influential leaders and visionaries in your particular ethnic, racial, or religious group.

Encourage Closeness

5. Teach the value of friendship by welcoming your kids' friends into your home. Encourage sleepovers. When possible, include their friends in your family outings and vacations. Do more than just take the friends along: show interest in their lives and in their families, and share of yourself with them. Open your home to your own friends and family, so your kids can see you valuing your own connections.

6. Are you comfortable having the kids around, listening and watching while you and your spouse or partner argue or disagree? If not, it may be a sign that you're not proud of your conflict-resolution skills. Many of us aren't. If your skills need improvement, take a class or workshop, or schedule several sessions with a counselor. Your kids need to learn from you—who else will teach them?—how to disagree respectfully and fairly; they need to see that conflict, effectively dealt with, brings people closer in the end. The skills they pick up by watching (and imitating) you will impact their lives forever.

Value Loving Kindness

7. Children are never too young to participate in acts of loving kindness. Turn birthdays and holidays into times for giving, not just receiving. Help your kids deliver the toys they've outgrown to a day care center or children's hospital—don't just do it for them. Volunteer together at a food pantry or animal shelter. Kids can practice loving kindness through the compassionate care of an animal and through babysitting younger children.

8. Be sure your children know about and witness your own acts of loving kindness. Talk with them about the charities you support, and ask for suggestions from them about worthy causes. Make a point of telling them when you've looked in on a suffering neighbor or family member, and enlist their help—chopping the onions, adding the chocolate chips—when you make a pot of soup or a batch of cookies for a sick friend.

Impart Gratitude

9. Model gratitude for your children by commenting frequently on the blessings in your life, especially during the tougher, challenging times when we tend to focus on the negative. Create a mealtime ritual, weekly or nightly, where each family member names one or two things that went well that day, one or two things for which they are grateful. Children as young as three or four can be taught to participate in this activity. Bedtime, too, can include a ritual in which parent and child together review the events of the day and acknowledge what there is to be thankful for. "What went well today?"

10. Gently denying our children some of the things they ask for is more likely to foster gratitude, than giving them so much that they come to expect that life's bounty is limitless. The fact that you may give yourself, materially, most of the things you want does not mean you should do the same for your kids. You may have earned it; they have not.

Imbue Spirituality

11. Model spirituality for your children by demonstrating—not just saying—that you value heart and soul—in them, in yourself, in friends and family. Talk admiringly about love, forgiveness, respect, kindness and compassion wherever you find it.

12. Regardless of whether your children raise the questions, you can do so yourself, casually, around the dinner table: questions

about the invisible world, about birth and death and good and evil. Draw the kids out; find out how their minds tackle these ideas. Conversations like these promote the development of a spiritual life.

13. See that your family calendar includes rituals—weekly, monthly, annually—and use those occasions to talk about the deeper meaning behind the day. Include plenty of sensory elements that children find so appealing—foods, colors, lights, sounds—and that will create warm and powerful memories to last a lifetime. Your kids' participation in richly meaningful rituals will promote a joyful place of spirituality in their lives.

Model Optimism

14. Teach your children that change can be good, that it can open up unexpected and wonderful possibilities. It's an attitude that promotes an optimistic stance toward the change that is inevitable in all our lives.

15. Promote optimism in your child by giving voice to philosophies of resilience: "There's no problem we can't handle," or "That which doesn't kill me makes me stronger." Convey message like these when they're young. Expose them to books like *The Little Engine That Could* and biographies about people who have persisted in the face of tough challenges.

16. Occasionally, at the dinner table, ask your children to name some small frustrations, disappointments, or setbacks that happened to them recently, as well as some big frustrations or set-

backs. Talk about how we know the difference between what's big and what's small, and how our responses to those two categories ought to differ.

Nurture Gratifying Pursuits

17. Do what you can to encourage your children's natural talents and interests, especially those that exercise key signature strengths. Take the online Signature Strengths Inventory with your kids and together review and discuss the results. Help them find hobbies, classes, summer camps, and after school programs that support their interests and strengths.

18. Two or three times a year, pull out photo albums or scrapbooks and gather the kids around to reminisce, reliving and savoring through memory the most enjoyable times.

Build Connectedness

19. Promote connectedness by listening to your kids, paying serious attention to what's on their minds. If you need to, ask questions to draw them out—when you're driving them to a friend's, while you're fixing dinner and they meander through the kitchen. Listen without advising, without criticizing, without helping. (There's time for that later.) Remember how effective empathy can be in helping them feel safe and understood, and in encouraging them to open up with you. And don't forget to share of yourself with them; it's not a one-way street. If *your* inner life—hopes and dreams, fears and disappoint-

ments—is completely closed off from them, don't be surprised if they close theirs off from you.

20. Have dinner with your children as often as you can. Few other activities offer as good an opportunity to show interest in their lives. Dinnertime together is a powerful way for kids to feel nurtured and cared for by you, no matter how old they are; it doesn't matter if the meal is homemade or brought in. Research shows that *not* eating dinner as a family raises your children's risk two- or three-fold for early sex, drug use, and emotional problems.

21. It's not unusual anymore for parents to be as plugged in as their kids to TV screens and computer monitors. The problem isn't so much what you are doing as what you're *not*: conversations, meals, outings, any activity where you're engaged side-by-side. Consider reading some of the books your middle- and high-schoolers are assigned in their English or literature classes. Discuss the books with them at dinner or when you're driving in the car, not as a quiz on what they know, but as a means of feeling close by sharing their experience.

Cherish Play

22. Don't be afraid of boredom. Don't think you need to remedy your kids' bored moments with a buffet of activity choices. "I'm bored" often serves as the prelude to the exercise of imagination and creativity, an opportunity for play. "I'm bored" offers our kids a chance to practice reflection, which is how they learn about themselves, how they visualize the future, how

they rehearse, in their minds, some of the challenges that lay ahead.

23. Limit the amount of time your kids sit in front of a computer monitor or TV screen becoming high-stimulation junkies, getting hooked on constantly changing scenes, fast action, bright colors and quirky sounds. True play requires time and space and the absence of distracting background noise, so our kids can hear themselves think, can hear the wheels of their own imagination turning.

Require Practice and Mastery

24. Join in as a kind of cheerleader on those occasions when your son or daughter, engaged in some activity, reaches the point of extreme frustration and wants to throw in the towel. Acknowledge their frustration while you commend their perseverence thus far. "Maybe I can help you figure out that hard part," you can offer when assembling the short-wave radio has severely tried your son's patience. "Why don't you keep at it for a little while longer," you can suggest, "and then let's go out for an ice-cream cone to celebrate your hard work."

Offer Recognition

25. Be generous with your recognition but don't flood your child with praise. Youngsters can become too dependent on the approval of others and lose the capacity for quiet, private *self-*approval. Occasionally, when your son or daughter approaches you and says, "How did I do?" ask first how *they* think they

did, a self-evaluation. After they've given an adequate re-sponse, add your two cents' worth of recognition.

Teach Self-Control

26. Set an example of self-control for your children. Deny your-self in the face of temptation, and let your children see it. "That jacket in the window is so nice, but I don't really need it." Or, "I'd really like a new car stereo, but it's not in the budget." Do the same with food—"That sundae looks delicious, but I've had enough to eat"—and with frustration in general—"It's no pleas-ure waiting in this long line, but we'll make the best of it."

Permissions

The authors are grateful for permission to include the following previously copyrighted material:

Excerpts from *The Childhood Roots of Adult Happiness* by Edward M. Hallowell, M.D., copyright © 2002 by Edward M. Hallowell, M.D. Used by permission of Ballantine Books, a division of Random House, Inc.

Excerpts from *Social Intelligence: The new science of human relationships* by Daniel Goleman, Ph.D., copyright © 2006 by Daniel Goleman, Ph.D. Used by permission of Bantam Books, a division of Random House, Inc.

Excerpt from *Excellence Without A Soul: How a Great University Forgot Education* by H.R.Lewis, copyright © 2006 by H.R.Lewis. Used by permission of the Perseus Book Group.

Excerpts from *The Blessing of a Skinned Knee* by Wendy Mogel, copyright © 2001 by Wendy Mogel, Ph.D. Used by permission of Simon & Schuster Publishing Group.

Acknowledgments

This book found its initial inspiration in the lecture "Why Good Homes Don't Produce Good Children" by educator, writer, and radio talk-show host Dennis Prager. It was Prager's observation that when children were asked what their parents wanted them most to be—good, smart, successful, or happy—their answer was typically "happy." We were fascinated by the fact that so many children were getting the message that happiness was *the most important thing,* and thus began the journey that culminated in this book.

We wish to thank the following people whose comments and suggestions about our manuscript helped us immeasurably along the way: A. Rachael Cunningham, M.S.W., Mary Doheny, Ph.D., Kama Einhorn, Allan Gold, Ph.D., Edward M. Hallowell, M.D., Merle Keitel, Ph.D., Richard Keitel, Maida Cohen LaMell, Jim McGowan, Sharon McGowan, David Myers, Ph.D., Barbara Rockman, Ph.D., Antoinette Saunders, Ph.D., Janet Weber, and Jay Zimbler.

Endnotes

[1] Kindlon, D. (2001). *Too much of a good thing: Raising children of character in an indulgent age.* New York: Hyperion. Kindlon reports on the Parenting Practices at the Millennium study, a large-scale survey of teenagers and parents across the United States that he and his research associates conducted during the late 1990s.

[2] Centers for Disease Control and Prevention. (2004, May 21). *Surveillance Summaries. MMWR, 53,* NSS-2, p.8

[3] Osberg, T.M. (2004, September 1). A business case for increasing college mental health services: increasing counseling services can increase student retention rates—and ultimately a college's bottom line. *Behavioral Health Management.*

[4] We wish to acknowledge the contribution of Harriette Unger to the discussion of why the happiness creed has been so widely embraced in recent decades.

[5] Edelman, G.N. (2006). How happy are your kids? *Familycircle.com.* New York: Meredith Corporation.

[6] Pew Research Center. (2006, February 13). "Are we happy yet?" A social trends report of the Pew Research Center. *www.pewresearch.org.*

[7] Frank, R.H. (2004). How not to buy happiness. *Daedalus, 133,* 2.

[8] Hallowell, E. M. (2002). *The childhood roots of adult happiness.* New York: Ballantine Books. p.4.

[9] Crossen, C.. (2006, March 6). Whether people define themselves as happy depends on the era. *Wall Street Journal.*

[10] McMahon, D.M. (2006). *Happiness: A history.* New York: Atlantic Monthly Press.

[11] Sondheim, S. (1987). *Into the woods.* Theatre Communications Group.

[12] Prager, D. Why good homes don't produce good children. Lecture available on audiotape at *www.stores.dennisprager.com.*

[13] Survey administered to 93 middle school students in March, 2006, at the Bernard Zell Anshe Emet Day School, Chicago, Illinois.

[14] Prager, D. (1998). *Happiness is a serious problem: A human nature repair manual.* New York: HarperCollins.

[15] Seligman, M.E.P. (2002). *Authentic happiness.* (New York: Free Press). p.118.

[16] Lambert, C. quotes D. Gilbert in The science of happiness. (2007, January-February). *Harvard Magazine.*

[17] Hallowell, E. *Op. cit.* p.220.

[18] Goleman, D. (1995). *Emotional intelligence: Why it can matter more than IQ.* New York: Bantam.

[19] Rosenthal, N. (2002). *The emotional revolution: How the new science of feelings can transform your life.* New York: Kensington Publishing.

[20] Layard, R. (2003, March). The secrets of happiness. *New Statesman.*

[21] Levine, M. (2006). *The price of privilege.* New York: HarperCollins.

[22] Conroy, P. and B. Johnston. (1991). *The prince of tides.* Screenplay of the film produced and directed by Barbra Streisand for Columbia Pictures.

[23] We say that thought *tends* to precede action so as not to overlook the whole category of behavioral responses to deep emotional triggers. Many triggers are outside of our awareness, and our responses to them are often automatic, fast, and seem to circumvent the conscious thought process.

[24] American Academy of Pediatrics. (2007). Some things you should know about preventing teen suicide. *www.aap.org.*

[25] Girls, Inc. (2006, October 12). The supergirl dilemma: Girls feel the pressure to be perfect, accomplished, thin, and accommodating. *www.girlsinc.org.*

[26] Edelman, G.N. *Op. cit.*

[27] Kindlon, D. *Op. cit.* p.23

[28] Goleman, D. (2006). *Social intelligence: The new science of human relationships.* New York: Bantam. p. 183.

[29] General Social Survey 1972-2004. Reported by Pew Research Center, *Op. cit.* p.2.

[30] Myers, D.G. (2000, January). The funds, friends, and faith of happy people. *American Psychologist, 55,* 1, 56-67.

[31] Inglehart, R. (1990). *Culture shift in advanced industrial society.* Princeton: Princeton University Press.

[32] Regan, T. (2004, December 15). Happiness. SRBI Public Affairs. *www.srbi.com/time_poll_arc11.html*

[33] Pew Research Center. *Op. cit.*

[34] Lykken, D. (1999). *Happiness.* New York: Golden Books. p.17.

[35] Argyle, M. (1987). *The psychology of happiness.* London: Methuen & Co.

[36] Brickman, P. et al. (1978). Lottery winners and accident victims: Is happiness relative? *Journal of Personality and Social Psychology, 36,* 917-927.

[37] Frey, B.S. and Stutzer, A. (2002). *Happiness and economics: How the economy and institutions affect human well-being.* Princeton: Princeton University Press.

[38] Happiness grows on trees: attitudes of the wealthy. (2001, May 1). *American Demographics.*

[39] Van Boven, L. and Gilovich, T. (2003). To do or to have? That is the question. *Journal of Personality and Social Psychology, 85(6)*, 1193-1202.

[40] Dey, E. L., Astin, A.W., and Korn, W.S. (1991). *The American freshman: Twenty-five year trends.* Los Angeles: Higher Education Research Institute, UCLA.

[41] Irvine, M. (2007, January 22). U.S. youths' priority: strike it rich. *Chicago Tribune.* Reporting on the Higher Education Research Institute (UCLA) study, The American freshman: National norms for 2006.

[42] Pew Research Center. (2007, January 9). How young people view their lives, futures and politics: a portrait of 'Generation Next.' *www.pewresearch.org.*

[43] Myers, D.G. *Op. cit.* p. 61

[44] Kasser, T. and Ryan, R.M. (1993). A dark side of the American dream: Correlates of financial success as a central life aspiration. *Journal of Personality and Social Psychology, 65*, 410-422.

[45] Mogul, W. (2001). *The blessing of a skinned knee: Using Jewish teachings to raise self-reliant children.* New York: Penguin. p.39

[46] Levine, M. *Op cit.*

[47] Kindlon, D. Lecture on February 1, 2007 at Frances Xavier Warde School, Chicago, IL.

[48] Mogul, W. *Op cit.* p.42.

[49] Iyengar, S.S. and Lepper, M.R. (1999). Rethinking the value of choice: A cultural perspective on intrinsic motivation. *Journal of Personality and Social Psychology, 76*, 349-366.

[50] Nigeria tops happiness survey. (2003, October 2). BBC News. *www.news.bbc.co.uk/go/pr/fr/-/1/hi/world/africa/3157570.stm*

[51] Gilbert, D.T. et al. (1998). Immune neglect: a source of durability bias in affective forecasting. *Journal of Personality and Social Psychology, 75*, 617-638.

[52] Lawson, W. (2005, May-June). Happiness? Mostly, we're born with it. *Psychology Today.*

[53] Goleman, D. *Social intelligence. Op. cit.* p.151

[54] *Ibid.* p 152

[55] Michalos, A. (2004). Social indicators research and health-related quality of life research. *Social Indicators Research, 65,* 27-72.

[56] Pew Research Center. *Op cit.* p.8

[57] Gilbert, D. (2006). *Stumbling on happiness.* New York: Knopf. p.20

[58] Seligman, M.E.P. (1975). *Helplessness: On depression, development, and death.* San Francisco: Freeman.

[59] Layard, R. (2005). *Happiness: Lessons from a new science.* New York: Penguin. Layard is analyzing data from the UK National Child Development Study.

[60] *Ibid.* p.181

[61] Niven, D. (2000). *The 100 simple secrets of happy people.* New York: Harper-Collins. p.2. Niven is citing H. Lepper (1996), "In pursuit of happiness and satisfaction in later life: a study of competing theories of subjective well-being." Ph.D. diss., University of California, Riverside.

[62] Hallowell, E. *Op cit.* p.18

[63] Seligman, M.E.P. (1988, October). Boomer blues. *Psychology Today.* 50-55.

[64] Myers, D.G. *Op cit.*

[65] Cohen, S. as quoted by D. Goleman in *Social intelligence. Op cit.* p. 247.

[66] Diener, E. and Seligman, M. E. P. (2002). Very happy people. *Psychological Science, 13,* 80-83.

[67] Pressman, S. D., Cohen, S., Miller, G. E., Barkin, A., Rabin, B. S., and Treanor, J. J. et al. (2005). Loneliness, social network size, and immune response to influenza vaccination in college freshmen. *Health Psychology, 24 (3),* 297-306.

[68] Demir, M. and Urberg, K., A. (2004). Friendship and adjustment among adolescents. *Journal of Experimental Child Psychology, 88,* 68-82.

[69] O'Connor, B. (1995). Family and friend relationships among older and younger adults. *International Journal of Aging and Human Development,* 40:9.

[70] The work of J.Cacioppo and G. Berntson is discussed by D. Goleman in *Social Intelligence. Op. cit.* p.10.

[71] Pew Research Center study. *Op cit.*

[72] Lyubomirsky, S., Sheldon, K.M., and Schkade, D. (2005). Pursuing happiness: the architecture of sustainable change. *Review of General Psychology, 9* (2), 111-131.

[73] Emmons, R. A.and McCullough, M. E. (2003). Counting blessings versus burdens: An experimental investigation of gratitude and subjective well-being in daily life. *Journal of Personality and Social Psychology, 84,* 377-389.

[74] Seligman, M. E. P., Steen, R. A., Park, N., and Peterson, C. (2005). Positive psychology progress: Empirical validation of interventions. *American Psychologist, 60,* 410-421.

[75] Crist-Houran, M. (1996). Efficacy of volunteerism. *Psychological Reports, 79:*736.

[76] Rilling, J.K., Gutman, D.A., Zeh, T.R., Pagnoni, G., Berns, G.S., and Kilts, C.D. (2002, July 18). A neural basis for social cooperation. *Neuron, 35,* 395-405.

[77] Bentham, J. Written June 22, 1830 and quoted in B. Parekh (ed.), (1993). *Jeremy Bentham: Critical Assessments.* (London: Routledge.) Vol. I. p.xvii.

[78] Emmons, R.A., and McCullough, M.E. Highlights from the research project on gratitude and thankfulness: Dimensions and perspectives of gratitude. *www.psychology.ucdavis.edu/labs/emmons/*

[79] Seligman, M.E.P. et al.(2005). *Op. cit.*

[80] Prager, D. *Op. cit.*

[81] Csikszentmihalyi, M. (1999, October). If we are so rich, why aren't we happy? *American Psychologist, 54*, 821-827.

[82] Gallup, G.G., Jr. (1984, March). Commentary on the state of religion in the U.S. today. *Religion in America: The Gallup Report*, No. 222.

[83] Layard, R. (2003, March 5). What would make a happier society? Lionel Robbins Memorial Lecture No.3 at the London School of Economics. *www.lse.ac.uk/collections/LSEPublicLecturesAndEvents/events/2003/20030106t1 439z001.htm*

[84] Hallowell, E. *Op. cit.* p.215.

[85] Inglehart, R. (1990). *Culture shift in advanced industrial society.* Princeton: Princeton University Press.

[86] Ellison, C.G. (1991). Religious involvement and subjective well-being. *Journal of Health and Social Behavior, 32*, 80-99.

[87] McIntosh, D.N., Silver, R.C., and Wortman, C.B. (1993). Religion's role in adjustment to a negative life event: coping with the loss of a child. *Journal of Personality and Social Psychology, 65*, 812-821.

[88] National Study of Youth and Religion. (2002, December 4). Sociologists find that religious teens are more positive about life. *www.youthandreligion.org/news/12-4-2002.html*

[89] Kushner, H. (1987, December). You've got to believe in something. *Redbook*, 92-94.

[90] Hallowell, E. *Op. cit.* p.51.

[91] Niven, D. *Op. cit.* Niven summarizes a finding from Lyubomirsky, S. (1994), "The hedonistic consequences of social comparison: implications for endur-

ing happiness and transient mood." PhD diss, Stanford University, Palo Alto, CA.

[92] Seligman, M.E.P. (2004, Spring). Can happiness be taught? *Daedalus*. Cambridge, MA: MIT Press.

[93] Seligman, M.E.P. (1996). *The optimistic child*. New York: HarperPerennial.

[94] Taylor, S.E. and J.D.Brown. (1988). Illusion and well-being: A social-psychological perspective on mental health. *Psychological Bulletin, 103*, 193-210.

[95] Clark, F., Carlson, M., Zemke, R., Gelya, F., Patterson, K., and Ennevor, B.L. (1996). Life domains and adaptive strategies of a group of low income, well older adults. *American Journal of Occupational Therapy 50*:99.

[96] Niven, D. *Op. cit.* Niven summarizes the findings of K. Panos (1997), Linking: an exploration of related constructs and effects on happiness. Master's thesis, American University, Washington, D.C.

[97] Seligman, M.E.P. (1996). *The optimistic child*. New York: Harper Perennial. p.98.

[98] Csikszentmihalyi, M. (1990). *Flow: The psychology of optimal experience*. New York: HarperPerennial.

[99] Seligman, M.E.P. (2002) *Authentic happiness. Op. cit.*

[100] Kindlon, D. *Op cit.* p.49.

[101] We acknowledge the contribution of Edward Hallowell, MD, whose distinguished book, *The Childhood Roots of Adult Happiness*, examines in greater depth many of the ideas set out in Part Three.

[102] Pieper, M.H. and Pieper, W.J.. (1999). *SmartLove*. Boston: The Harvard Common Press.

[103] *Ibid.* p.202

[104] Perry, B. (2002, April). Childhood experience and the expression of genetic potential: What childhood neglect tells us about nature and nurture. *Brain and Mind, 3* (1), 79-100.

[105] Goleman, D. *Social intelligence. Op. cit.* p. 182. Goleman is quoting from a personal communication with neuroscientist Richard Davidson.

[106] Field, T. (1998). Maternal depression effects on infants and early interventions. *Preventive Medicine, 27* (2), 200-203.

[107] Furstenberg, F. and Kiernan, K. (2001). Delayed parental divorce: How much do children benefit? *Journal of Marriage and the Family, 63,* 446-57.

[108] Amato, P., Loomis, L., and Booth, A. (1995). Parental divorce marital conflict, and offspring well-being during early adulthood. *Social Forces, 73,* 895-915.

[109] Various studies based on the data from the National Longitudinal Study of Adolescent Health can be found at:
www.cpc.unc.edu/projects/addhealth/pubs?makePrintable=1&style=1038

[110] Goodnow, C. (2002, October 29). Science offers parents clues on how to help their children build a good life. *Seattle Post-Intelligencer.*

[111] Hofferth, S.L. (1999). Changes in children's time 1981-1997. *Center Survey, 9,* no.1.

[112] Edelman, G.N. *Op. cit.*

[113] Levine, M. *Op cit.* p.32

[114] Council of Economic Advisers. Teens and their parents in the 21st century: an examination of the trends in teen behavior and the role of parental involvement. *www.clinton4.nara.gov/media/pdf/CEAreport.pdf*

[115] Edelman, G. *Op. cit.*

[116] Kaiser Family Foundation. (2003, October). Zero to six: electronic media in the lives of infants, toddlers and preschoolers. *www.kff.org/entmedia/3378.cfm*

[117] Eisenberg, M., et al. (2004). Correlations between family meals and psychosocial well-being among adolescents. *Archives of Pediatrics and Adolescent Medicine, 158,* 792-96.

[118] Hallowell, E. *Op cit.* p.103

[119] Williams, A. (May 20, 2007). Putting the skinned knees back into playtime. *New York Times.*

[120] Hofferth, S. *Op cit.*

[121] Goleman, D. *Social intelligence. Op. cit.* p.180

[122] Hallowell, E. *Op cit.* p. 221.

[123] Goleman, D. quotes R. Davidson in *Social intelligence, Op. cit.* p. 185.

[124] Hallowell, E. *Op. cit.* p. 147

[125] Mueller, C. M. and Dweck, C.S. (1998). Praise for intelligence can undermine children's motivation and performance. *Journal of Personality and Social Psychology. 75(1),* 33-52.

[126] Bronson, P. (2007, February). How not to talk to your kids: The inverse power of praise. *New York Magazine. http://nymag.com/news/features/27840/*

[127] Kula, I. (2006). Lecture at North Shore Center for the Performing Arts, Skokie, IL.

[128] Kindlon, D. February 1, 2007 lecture, *Op. cit.*

[129] Newman, S. (2006, October 11). Are you a "yes" parent? *New York Metro Parents Magazine.*

[130] Lewis, H. R. (2006). *Excellence without a soul: how a great university forgot education.* New York: PublicAffairs.

[131] *Time.* May 15, 2006.

AARON COOPER began his professional life as a high school psychology teacher before becoming a clinical psychologist. In the late seventies, he was a member of the child and adolescent program at Ravenswood Community Mental Health Center in Chicago. In 1985, he joined the department of psychiatry at Kaiser Permanente in San Francisco, where he was on staff for eighteen years. In addition to a private practice, he lectured, taught and consulted throughout Northern California on the topics of child and family therapy, brief strategic therapy, and couples communication. Aaron holds a B.A. from Harvard, a Masters in Teaching from Northwestern, and a doctorate from Loyola University of Chicago. He is currently the director of FamilyMattersOnline, a project of the Family Institute at Northwestern University.

ERIC KEITEL left a career in medicine in 1991 to pursue his lifelong interest in education. From 1992 to 1996, he was a teacher and Director of Family Education at Brandeis Hillel Day School in San Francisco. After one year as Head of School of the Jewish Day School of Sonoma County, he was named Founding Head of Middle School at Hausner Day School in Palo Alto, a position he held until 2001. Since 2003, he has served as Director of Family Education at Bernard Zell Anshe Emet Day School in Chicago. Eric holds a B.A. from the State University of New York at Binghamton, a Masters in Educational Administration from San Francisco State, and a certificate in educational leadership from the Harvard Graduate School of Education Principals' Center.